Awake

My Soul

Timothy Jones

Doubleday

New York   London   Toronto

Sydney   Auckland

$\mathscr{A}$ wake
My Soul

PRACTICAL SPIRITUALITY
FOR BUSY PEOPLE

PUBLISHED BY DOUBLEDAY, a division of Random House, Inc.
1540 Broadway, New York, New York 10036

DOUBLEDAY and the portrayal of an anchor with a dolphin are
trademarks of Doubleday, a division of Random House, Inc.

Book design by Maria Carella
Illustration by Louis Jones

Library of Congress Cataloging-in-Publication Data
Jones, Timothy K., 1955–
Awake my soul / Timothy Jones. — 1st ed.
p.   cm.
1. Spiritual life—Christianity.   I. Title.
BV4501.2.J659   1999
248.4—dc21   98–38357
CIP

ISBN 0-385-49156-5

Printed in the United States of America

April 1999

First Edition

1   3   5   7   9   10   8   6   4   2

CONTENTS

Acknowledgments   *vii*

Introduction   *ix*

Chapter 1
YOU DON'T HAVE TO BE A SAINT   *1*

Chapter 2
GOD WITHIN REACH   23

Chapter 3
WAYS WE WAKE   47

Chapter 4
EYES AND EARS OPEN   67

Chapter 5
THE SOUL AND THE SIMPLE LIFE   87

Chapter 6
EVERYDAY RHYTHMS   *107*

Chapter 7
WAKING UP TO MORE THAN A JOB   *125*

Chapter 8
SOUL COMPANIONS   *141*

Chapter 9
THE HARD, HIDDEN GRACES OF SUFFERING   *159*

Chapter 10
FACING OUR FRAGILITY   *177*

Chapter 11
AWAKE TO THE FACES AROUND US   *195*

Chapter 12
BY FITS AND STARTS   *213*

Afterword   225

End Notes   227

ACKNOWLEDGMENTS

I am grateful to those who read portions of the manuscript and offered insightful critique: Hunter Moore, Peter Shockey, Steve Wilburn, and Jill Zook-Jones.

I am also indebted to the insights of Eugene Peterson and Christopher de Vinck, whose influence and writings have enriched me immeasurably.

My agent, Margaret Langstaff, and Mark Fretz and Eric Major at Doubleday also merit my hearty thanks for making this book possible.

INTRODUCTION

How many common things are trodden under foot
which, if examined carefully, awaken our astonishment.
AUGUSTINE

One early evening I sat at home, working at my desk. Outside my window the sun lit up the yard's maple and elm trees and made the lawn a luminous green. With the lengthening days, anyone could tell that a Tennessee spring was turning into summer. But none of that pried my eyes off the project on my desk.

What did it was my then-five-year-old daughter, Bekah. She stood on the grass with thin arms stretched toward the sun, her eyes squinting, her chestnut hair shimmering. Then she ran and skipped and twirled around the yard, laughing with abandon. I could barely hear her through the window, but I could see her clearly. I became a witness to her sheer delight in living, her immersion in the glories of the moment.

Bekah had no idea I was watching—and taking notes. "Seeing Bekah awakened in me," I later wrote in my journal, "a moment of admiration and longing." I admired her exuberance. I longed to trade in my businesslike ways for some of her childlike wonder. The daughter I was trying so hard to raise, a kindergartner who could barely read, was teaching me.

I did not take long to return to the project on my desk—I was, after all, up against a deadline. The publisher who had hired me expected my editing job to come in on time. Given my profession, when I am not helping get others in my household out the door for jobs, or helping with their school work, I edit others' work and write my own. But I stored my glimpse of Bekah in my mind. And I still come back to it, still replay it. For I see in her childlike play possibilities for how I live. In the thick (and thin) of my everyday circumstances I want to stay awake to the marvel of life. "Lately," someone writes, echoing my longing, "I have begun to wonder if it is still possible to taste the world up close as I did as a child."[1] How can I cultivate more delight in what matters? I long to notice—really notice—the faces of people around me. And I grow more eager to run after my soul's desire for God. I want what I saw in Bekah to stay with me. After all, if a glimpse of Bekah skipping around the yard can teach me, what other prospects might await, hidden in plain sight?

I think of other times that something nudged me from my dullness. These momentary awakenings happen sometimes when I least expect them. Sometimes when I am too involved or tired to expect anything at all. Sometimes smack in the midst of what someone calls life's "grubby particulars." My eyes open to what, before, maybe I missed.

So I stir awake in a hotel room outside of Nashville, not long after the May evening I caught a glimpse of Bekah. I've been roused by the sunlight filtering through the shades into the room, or perhaps the murmurs of my family's breathing through their heavy sleep. It's my forty-second birthday, our first day of summer vacation, and Abram, his six-foot-two frame stretched along the next bed, snores. Bekah sprawls on the sofa next to our bed, her tiny barrel of ribs rising and falling with each gentle breath. Jill, next to me, turns and drowsily moves closer. I had had a hectic week getting ready to leave work, but while they all sleep I think, *What gifts they are!* Now more than my eyelids and limbs wake up. A wave of gratefulness washes over me.

These moments of everyday awakening happen during mundane days on the job, too. Once I was driving to the publishing office where I worked, knowing a stressful day awaited me. But as I drove, I tried to think about seeing God's hand in the day about to unfold. I said good morning to the office manager as I walked to my desk and flipped on my computer. A normal day began. But it was also different; I tried to look up from my desk through the day. I don't just mean physically, simply in the tilt of the neck—but in the outlook of my soul, that faculty able to perceive life's larger dimensions. I took moments to lean back in my chair and enjoy the view of the Nashville skyline in the distance. I tried to listen with a "third ear" when I talked to people, to pick up not just what they said but also what they must be feeling. And through appointments and phone calls, I watched for traces of God in the corners and crevices of an ordinary nine-to-five. It was not a perfect day. But a *profound* one. At assorted moments I was *aware*. And that made all the difference.

In varied and sometimes haphazard ways I try to stop, look, listen, the way I was told to do as a child. I'm not an expert, but I listen for quiet truths that sometimes seem eloquent, other times barely whispered, and often muffled by distractions. I listen as I would for notes of music from a radio station, coming in faintly, competing with static, growing clearer as I near the signal's source. And I peel my eyes for what lies beneath the surface of so many everyday happenings. My senses come alive to a quiet, unseen Presence. Not so much in thunderclaps, but in the common things, the dust specks that make up any life. I try to watch even when I get tempted to yawn my way through the routine, when I think not much seems to happen.

"Life is one long process of getting tired," someone once wrote. I know what he means, some days. I get caught up in little crises. I get wearied from the demands. But I also know that resigning myself to mind-numbing busyness isn't the only option. What the ancients called *apetheia*, better known to us as apathy— not caring much about the abundance poured into our lives—need not define my outlook. At least not all the time. I make the prayer of the ancient psalm writer my own: "Awake, my soul." We say, perhaps only tentatively, at first only sporadically, "Let us awake, O God, to you, to others, to what matters." And that makes a difference.

But perhaps you consider yourself only modestly religious. Perhaps some difficult experience at the hands of "spiritual" people has left you wary. Or you may know all the words and beliefs, you have the customs down pat, but your faith feels drained dry, like a friend I had lunch with yesterday. When I asked him about his prayer life, he could only grimace and tell me that he longs for a more vibrant experience. From wherever you come, you want to find a God-aware way to move through routine.

Fortunately, the possibilities are wonderful. Our small beginnings take us somewhere. "Those who have shaken off sleep," wrote the second-century sage Clement of Alexandria, "eventually become all awake within." Clement spoke of an "eternal adjustment of vision" that allows us to see what before was only a blur. That suggests what can happen in every soul, each life, in all kinds of settings. Even when we feel hurried, hassled, and harried.

I am not talking about a magical release from life's disappointments and ordinary challenges, of course. But I am discovering the joy of tiny awakenings: while enduring the heartbreak of a loved one's rejection, talking to a neighbor, volunteering at a homeless shelter, even just sitting in a chair for a moment of quiet. What I see may be almost imperceptible, but it is real. Perhaps I am weeding a flower bed or taking a breather from the report I'm writing, and suddenly it seems as if something important is trying to make itself known. Or I spend a rainy Saturday morning reading in bed, grateful for the simple pleasure of losing myself in a story. Or something opens my eyes to the wonder of a smiling friend sitting across from me at a café table. I glimpse a deeper, spiritual dimension.

"I hear a rustling behind me or a whisper on the wind," Robert Benson writes of the divine presence, "detect a smile or a gesture between friends or lovers or strangers, touch a stone or blossom or the hand of my child—and it is there."[2] Perhaps you felt the presence as a child, but feel as if you've wandered away. As Avery Brooke roamed the hillside fields and through the woods near her home as a child, she writes, "I sensed something more, a presence, a power for which I had no explanation. What was it in the sweep of the sky, the giant outcropping of rock, the sassafras lead in my hand? I did not know, but I felt hushed by awe and quiet joy."[3] She lost that awareness for a time, only to find it again as an adult. Perhaps you, too, want to recover it, or truly discover it for the first time.

What I am after here is a spirituality of daily life, for real people. This is not about religion for its own sake—mere rules, duty, and custom. No, I have in mind seizing the times we spend at office or factory or school, sit at a table to eat a meal, flinch at news of a child's illness, even grieve over a parent's death. These are the settings where the soul makes its discoveries. This book explores ways of finding God at every turn.

I know that freighted words will sometimes get in the way of what I try to describe. People hear terms like *soul* and *spiritual* and they are apt to think only of heaven and angels, high ethical ideals, or doing good in a vaguely pleasant way. We forget how much faith can be woven into the details of life.

My brother Kevin, who has spent much of his religious passion in pursuit of the path of an Eastern-oriented guru, once told me, "I don't just want to think about God or talk about God. I want to *know* God. I want to experience it." I don't follow his path, but I understand the longing. "Better to see the face than hear the name," an Asian proverb goes. Better truly to glimpse God than merely to play at religion or just go through the routines. Why be a distant observer when more is possible?

I recall an early morning when I'm getting ready for work: I hear Jill and Abram out in the kitchen, talking in the hushed tones of early morning, pulling down the boxes of breakfast cereal, jangling the silverware drawer, setting bowls on the maple tabletop. Meanwhile I pull on my pants, I spray on cologne, hurriedly trying to get ready. I'm due at the office at eight and I've been late a couple of times already this week. Rushing around gets me harried. But then my mind slows down. My soul stirs. I have a "God-moment" with a thought so unformed you could barely call it a prayer. But it is. A warm sensation fills me. What I'm doing becomes—fleetingly, but no less profoundly—an experience of God's presence. Life has a sense of being in place.

Times like these make us aware of Something More—Some*one* More. "The experience," Quaker Thomas Kelly wrote, "is of an invasion from beyond, of an Other who in gentle power breaks in upon our littleness and in tender expansiveness makes room for Himself."[4] Isn't that what we seek? "Implosions of grace," a friend calls such flashes. Our life becomes more than it was when we tried on our own.

What I describe in this book has to do with both ancient wisdom and contemporary experience. With each day, it seems, our interest in soul matters grows. After decades of embarrassed silence, spirituality is out of the closet, I once read, and within arm's reach at any supermarket checkout aisle, right along with Chap Stick and breath mints. From tabloids to high-fashion magazines, interest in angels and the afterlife won't go away. Books on nonthreatening Buddhist "mindfulness" attract people who have little interest in the trappings of Eastern religious culture. Monasteries find themselves booked months in advance as seekers pour in for personal retreats. Stories of miracles intrigue millions of TV viewers. Every indicator says that our souls are hungry for more than pop psychology, amateur sociology, or impersonal technology. We want to do more than advance at the office, gratify our hormones, or become "integrated."

For all its potential for helping us understand ourselves, even the much-talked-about idea of "emotional intelligence" only goes so far. We want a "*spiritual* intelligence," a savvy about the issues of life that cannot be measured in gross income or hard disk space.

But what will it look like in real life? We feel in a half-guilty way that we should be more spiritually anchored, but while we already know what is needed, we lack the spiritual wherewithal. How in the world do you maintain a vivid sense of the sacred when bombarded by urgent faxes and the demands of headstrong teen-agers? And is the spiritual life practical? If you are not a monk or closet mystic, can you even hope to live with daily spiritual aware-ness? You don't want to move to a remote cabin in the woods or face an exhausting regimen. "I work at an office," a friend says, "and I'm the father of four children, so my life is full of child care, homework help, and handyman jobs around the house. I want to be able to find God in the ordinary parts of life, but I know it won't be easy."

Well, it's *not* always easy. Waking up spiritually, like rousing a tired body from bed when we'd rather sleep late, can be just plain hard. We may expend great effort. But something in us *already* wants to get up, go deeper. I think of my friend Judith Smith, an "intensely workaholic" executive. Slowly, almost imperceptibly, the questions in her life kept turning "ever more toward the soul." The experiences varied, she told me—"reading an author who seemed to articulate what was happening in me, hearing a speaker talk about prayer, praying the Psalms with friends and then sharing the silence. Finally I began to realize that the common thread running through all of these experiences was a growing awareness of my hunger for God—a deep hunger that is painful and wonderful at the same time." She found something stirring awake. She paid attention until she could rouse from sleep. Or let herself *be* roused.

That's what I explore in this book. Not abstract theory, but what I and others have discovered in real life. So in what follows I will regularly invite you into the scenes of my daily life. Not because my life is exceptional, but because I have learned to watch for, in the midst of a usually ordinary life of children, deadlines, and lower back pain, signs of Someone above—and beyond and within. What I experience cannot be exhaustively explained. But I can point. I can invite you to eavesdrop, standing by a cracked-open door to over-hear what God hints at and whispers to me and others, hearing for yourself the Voice that I—that most of us—long to hear. I suggest simple practices that have helped me. I share the stories of acquaintances. I gather words of those who over the centuries have committed their discoveries to writings.

While we stand to learn much, we need not feel intimidated by soul matters. This is not about getting crammed full with a hundred-and-one "to do's." As happens with any relationship, growing awareness of the Divine Other—and the others we rub shoulders with daily—means both wanting and waiting. Trying hard and not worrying too much. Seeking but also being found. We reach out but mostly let God grasp us. So I will suggest approaches to try, yet also leave you space to see and hear for yourself. To learn and grow as God leads.

A final note: I planned to limit myself to what has traditionally been called spirituality. I could have followed in the vein of the classic, *The Practice of the Presence of God,* written by a medieval monk named Brother Lawrence. But I realized as I wrote how much waking up to God also entails a waking up to the human faces around us. The two are of a piece. It is hard to pray and not hear some invitation to walk back into the scenes of daily living with something new to share with others. So while the accent will stay on the "spiritual," much of what I write will also apply to our living with our friends, neighbors, coworkers. I will explore what Jesus called the two great commandments: to love God with the whole self, and to love our neighbors as ourselves. The idea is to end up *more* connected to the gritty, joyful, everyday realities of normal life. Not less. The hope is to find in the soul's discoveries a staying power for life's tough relationships, for all of life's trying turns and detours.

I claim to have reached no spiritual pinnacle, but I have glimpsed discoveries that have changed my outlook and transformed my praying. Perhaps they will help you, as they have helped me, to demystify a topic that leaves many daunted and frustrated. The encounters and epiphanies I point to happen amid little moments and grand experiences. They can come to the depths of the heart and in the scenes of everyday life. And they can include you.

This is a book about letting that happen. Anyone can become more alert to what really matters. All of us can wake up to life's everyday signs and wayside wonders. Even a child can do it. Bekah, on that bright spring day, made me realize how beyond imagining the possibilities are.

Chapter 1

You Don't
HAVE TO BE
A SAINT

You turn us toward yourself through wondrous means.
AUGUSTINE

$O\!ne$ day, years ago, something simple and quiet nudged me awake.

I was hitting my teens, coping with the normal energies and anxieties of adolescence. Momentous events unfolded around me—assassinations, campus sit-ins, a draft that threatened to send my brother to Vietnam. But like nearly everyone else in my Southern California suburb in 1968, I lived an ordinary life. I thought mostly about everyday matters—friends, parents, life at Columbus Junior High.

But late one October afternoon as I walked home from school, the God of all things made his presence vividly felt. It was simple, really. I had been noticing how clearly I could see the craggy hills in the distance after an autumn wind swept the valley clean of smog. A yellowing sun cast long shadows on the sidewalk. The breezy coolness felt good on my cheeks. And I sensed with sudden elation that God was *there*. As I say, this was no complicated encounter; the clouds did not form themselves into a sky-written message from the

Great Beyond. I don't think I told anyone. But the childhood God I had lobbed prayers to, the being I had vaguely reverenced on Sundays, somehow became a compelling Presence. I knew deep in my soul, perhaps for the first time, that God *was*.

I couldn't foresee it then, but that encounter began to effect a change that would take years to fathom. Life went on in normal ways. I grew into an adult, moved East to attend grad school, met my future wife, fell out and reconciled with my parents, fathered children, changed careers more than once. But I found myself wondering about staying aware. How could I not lose track of the goodness that touched me that afternoon? Through the years, through the joys and things I cannot understand, I have tried to keep my eyes wide open. I have tried to listen to my soul's stirrings, those impulses I may brush past on a busy day.

For while I believe that there is no place where God is not, I sometimes overlook the Presence. Distractions and drowsy eyes keep me from seeing. It's right there, "under our noses," I once heard someone say. We live in a "God-bathed world," philosopher and writer Dallas Willard suggests.[1] But then I forget how spiritually rich even ordinary moments are, how precious the people with whom I rub shoulders. Only every now and then do most of us really see and hear with our souls. But at least some of the time we can stand before everyday wonders and not be preoccupied, not be so emotionally tired we forget to look. We can learn to heed our soul's best intuitions.

These daily awakenings arrive in great variety. "There are many kinds of awakening that God effects in the soul," wrote poet and priest John of the Cross centuries ago, "so many that we would never finish explaining them all."[2] They may come with palpable intensity while others may overtake us gently. I remember insights that came with the weight of a conversion, others as a bare touch. Awareness of God can come suddenly or gradually. Something tries to catch our attention, invites us to "look this way." And we want to respond. We want to *stay* awake.

Some years ago I saw the movie *Awakenings* (based loosely on the book by that title). The main character, played by Robert De Niro, suffers from a disorder that robs him of virtually all consciousness. He is left catatonic, almost comatose. He walks, he opens his eyes, he sees, but only in the vaguest way. Then a drug is found that helps De Niro awaken. Once again he notices people, especially his mother and an attractive young woman who frequents the hospital to visit her father. Now, when he opens his eyes, his whole self sees. He and his fellow patients rediscover dancing, talking, romancing. The ward rollicks with people given back their lives.

But the drug soon has intolerable side effects. The awakening doesn't last. De Niro descends again into the world of half-living, what looks to the outsider as being alive but asleep. It makes for a poignant ending.

When it comes to waking up spiritually, however, another way is possible. Our quiet experiences and "Aha!" moments lead somewhere. They need not be like a list of New Year's resolutions that sits in the bottom of a desk drawer, forgotten. In my experience, encountering God is an ongoing, unfolding way of life. What I describe in this book grows out of conversations with dozens of friends and even strangers, seeing up close how they tried, or failed and tried again. I write having ransacked the writings and stories of great souls through the centuries. I found that nothing less than a picture of a yawning soul shaking off sleep—again and again— captures the power of what can happen.

This is the promise of that October afternoon years ago in California when I felt overtaken by the sudden awareness of a Presence. This is the promise of your own life's ordinary and not-so-ordinary moments. In a kitchen, on the subway, sharing coffee with a neighbor, reading the paper on the backyard deck, it's possible not to miss God. Possible not to sleep through his appearing. Possible to live, because of that, with a God-graced awareness of others.

But how?

LET WAKING UP
HAPPEN NATURALLY, GENTLY

I remember one predawn Christmas morning when I was eleven. I had spent months fashioning homemade drums out of kitchen pans, stretching brown paper over the rims, holding the paper fast with rubber bands. My cymbals were pan lids. My drumsticks, chopsticks. I made primitive rhythm and my "drums" were inadequate. But this Christmas I expected my first real instrument—a snare drum. At dawn I sneaked out to our living room, long before anyone else was awake, and there it was. I touched its taut, sandpapery drum head, admired its chrome, felt the smooth hickory drumsticks, but only briefly, so as not to be caught snooping. I went back to bed, happy. Later, when the family called me out, shielding the drum with a blanket, then dropping it with a flourish to reveal the longed-for gift, I feigned surprise. But I had been long awake, watching. Natural curiosity and anticipation would not let me stay sleeping.

Something similar happens to our souls, our spirits—whatever you name that part of us that senses and responds to the Divine. "The simple desire for God is already the beginning of faith," I once read. Even in our souls' longing and wanting we are already beginning to wake up. No equipment is required save a seeking heart. "There is that near you," wrote an old Quaker seeker, "that will guide you. Wait for it, and be sure to keep to it." No matter if you feel out of practice.

Many things race through our minds each day; we want another promotion at the office, we cross our fingers that our kids turn out okay, we hope to stay healthy ourselves; but running even deeper is the longing for God. Sometimes I rush through my life's daily scenes, oblivious and insensitive. But in our deepest selves we want to go on. We stir awake because we suspect that we cannot get by without God. In most of us, writes one spiritual teacher, our heart "lies dormant and undeveloped. If it were awakened it would be constantly straining toward God and, given a chance, would impel the whole of our being toward him."[3] Our longing both propels and guides us. We simply pay attention and respond. We are the ones that make the search for spiritual reality daunting, not God. In the end, spirituality is giving ourselves permission to do what we most long to do. "God made us," C. S. Lewis once observed, "as a person invents an engine. A car is made to run on gasoline. . . . God designed the human machine to run on Himself. He Himself is the fuel our spirits were designed to burn."[4] It can be as natural as breathing. And is that essential.

When I neglect God, I find, my soul cries out, just as busy neglect of my stomach's pangs finally drives me to the refrigerator. Just as lack of exercise leaves my body flabby, restless. Just as my back lets me know when I sit for hours sloppily slumped in a chair. And when I go too many days without special stretching and strengthening exercises, I really pay. So it is with the inner life of the soul. Its aches drive me to spiritual relief. Our God-given desire to be stretched becomes a great ally in the soul's growth.

That gives us a great advantage. Developing a living soul is not like mastering a foreign language. This is not something you have to get a degree to "get." Writes Christopher de Vinck, "We *all* possess universal insights that, on the surface, appear to be just ordinary moments."[5] We mostly need to recognize them.

My friend Stephen Bryant, verging on burnout in a professional life that had him "passionate to change the world and remake my soul," realized he was trying to do it all on the strength of his own insight and energy. He was turning spiritual growth into a difficult project, as though he were running a spirituality business in a competitive market. So he got away to a retreat center in the desert.

His spiritual advisors there, the monks, asked, "Why have you come to the desert?"

"To learn what it means to pray and to love God," he responded.

"Do you love God?" they asked.

"I want to," Stephen replied.

"Well," he heard, "in your longing to love God you are already loving God."[6]

Stephen was finally able to stop making the spiritual life a superhuman achievement.

Make that shift and the climate changes dramatically.

LET WAKING UP HAPPEN IN THE THICK OF NORMAL, EVERYDAY LIFE

God usually doesn't ask us to move to another address, just to stay where we are long enough to see what He's doing, hear what He's saying. We turn to God while doing the laundry, not just as we pray in church. We trace His work in the moment, not just the momentous. After all, God met me on an October afternoon while I just walked home.

Such "everydayness" may come as a relief. "This shouldn't be a project I am going to have to add to an already crowded life," someone confessed. "This has to be something I can integrate into what I'm already doing." Who hasn't had days when coping with the nitty-gritty of a job, household duties, and family demands seemed more than enough—a great deal more than enough? And then to give sustained, focused attention to something else?

But words like *spiritual* don't have to signal a split between the everyday and eternal. Why make the sacred so ethereal that it has no connection with the secular? We are not talking here about what Evelyn Underhill calls "a fenced-off devotional patch rather difficult to cultivate, and needing to be sheltered from the cold winds of the outer world."[7] I'm discovering how *daily* spirituality usually is. How permeable the soul's longings can be to the routines of our vacuuming, taking the kids to school, working out at the gym. A serene woodland view is not the only setting for meditating on God. Reading the Bible doesn't require an unhurried afternoon with no children clamoring through the door or phone ringing. I look for traces of the Presence while carrying on as a middle-aged husband, aspiring writer, father who both jokes with and snaps at the kids, and a morning jogger who usually plods. What looks pretty ordinary is in fact gloriously ordinary.

Paul Nancarrow, a doctoral student and Episcopal priest I know, tells of an incident when his son was still a toddler:

> Aidan was busily riding his trike in our back yard. I was sitting out on the deck, reading a book. And for a moment I put it down. I looked up and began watching Aidan. I don't know what it was about that moment, but watching him playing, I had this tremendous flood of love for my son. I thought what an amazing, awe-inspiring thing it was that God should give such a wonderful little creature into our lives to watch over and enjoy, to get frustrated with and make up with. What a wonderful thing! I thought this must be a little bit of how God feels about Aidan. And a little bit of the love God has for me. It was a remarkable moment. It took my breath away. I got up, jumped off the deck and scooped Aidan up, and we played for a half-hour.

Nothing, not even busyness, need separate us from the love of God we long for. Not when God can be found in the midst of life itself. Amid office stresses and kitchen noise, I wait for hints and whispers of God. I commune with God in a supermarket checkout aisle as often as I do in predawn devotions.

So here is a man whose story pastor and writer Eugene Peterson tells. The man wanted help in thinking more about God as he went about his everyday activities. He would buy inexpensive Bibles, Peterson writes. At the start of the day he would rip out a fresh page and stick it in a shirt pocket. At odd moments he would pull it out, read a few lines, reflect, and then go on with what he was doing. The day over, he crumpled it up and threw it into the trash. I've never known anyone else to do that. But the man saw no reason not to integrate spirituality into the scenes of everyday life. I admire that.[8]

Not long ago I ran across this story, one that perhaps Eugene Peterson's friend might like: Some students asked their spiritual teacher to help them find God. "No one can help you do that," the elder said.

"Why not?" the disciples asked, amazed.

"For the same reason that no one can help fish to find the ocean."

You do not find God through fleeing the world, he might have continued; you find God all around you—already there, *where you live*.

I'm in morning traffic, late to work, angry at the sluggishness on a normally clear road. Stretching ahead as far as I can see is a backed-up river of cars. The lanes to my right and left are jammed. I am drumming my palms on the steering wheel, trying not to get more antsy.

But in my agitation I call to mind an ancient prayer I'm learning, part of which goes, "God be in my eyes, and in my looking." I say it slowly. Soon I realize what I'm asking. Wherever I am, whatever I'm doing, I am reaching for a different way to see. "God be in my heart, and in my thinking," it continues. I find my prayer being answered in the asking. I realize I can fixate on the harsh, unyielding concrete and steel. I can glare at people jockeying with me for a position in the traffic. Or I can see with different eyes, with an opened soul. I look around. And finally I glimpse other elements in the picture: leafy maples gracing the roadside, a cloudless September sky above. I watch the faces of my fellow travelers, some already weary, some dreaming about their days. They are honking, on cell phones, putting on makeup. And suddenly I see *persons,* not anxious motorists.

I have to fight impatience the rest of my trip, as it turns out. While I hate being late, I often cut time so short I have no margin. That habit is catching up with me today. But something is different. Right in the middle of a mundane and hurried and unexceptional situation, I have invited God in. *God be in my eyes.* A grind becomes grace. An irritating commute turns into an encounter. My car a sanctuary. I even find myself praying that my fellow motorists would experience God's calm. *God be in my heart.* And I tell myself, *Can't that happen more often, in the perennial irritations?*

"You turn us toward yourself by wondrous means," Augustine once prayed. He might have also said by *ordinary* means. Which means we learn to see our lives, even in their boredom and pain and exhilaration, as a meeting place with the God of the infinite universe. There we find Him, Lord of the little things of our universe. We learn to draw on resources that go deeper and beyond our own, but that become instantly practical.

I am on another trip, this time soaring thirty thousand feet aboveground, in a jet plane bound for Dallas. A slight "seepage" of fuel from the engine just before the scheduled takeoff required extra checks and a long delay. Now a low-lying cloud cover below us will make me even later. I'm hungry, tired, restless.

But suddenly through the plane's windows, a bright, late-afternoon sun glints off the gold accents of the pen I'm writing with. The cabin becomes suffused with a gentle light. I look at Jill, in the seat next to me, contentedly absorbed in her book. I realize these delays aren't postponing me from living life. This *is* life. And I try now to greet it with acceptance, with a willingness to look deeper.

As I sit waiting for the pilot to announce our clearance to land, I think about the saying: "Don't sweat the small stuff—and it's all small stuff." I guess the slogan (and book title) has an admirable intention: Try to whittle down the tensions that threaten to over-power you, or at least, like with me in a delayed plane, disturb your calm.

But the way to peace is not in my telling myself my schedule doesn't matter, or that my hungry, achy body is fooling me by its signals. No, the answer is to realize that *everything* matters. Nothing is insignificant, small stuff. Everything has potential to teach me. I see glimmers of God in ordinary, even frustrating moments. Even interruptions and delays can provide me moments of awareness. Even irritating people can provide me a chance to show compassion.

I'm long since off the plane as I write this. But today has its own challenges. Few things agitate me more than doing the year's taxes. Lately, I've spent too many evenings, for my taste, gathering records. But then it struck me this afternoon: Is what I'm saying about seeing more deeply through life's ordinary moments true or not? Nothing need be empty of purpose. Nothing is so common-place that it cannot provide ground for waking up. For nothing is devoid of the God who permeates and sustains everything. I'll try to remember that tonight when faced with my tax forms and disordered receipts.

Tom Schwanda teaches seminary classes in spiritual formation and administers programs for a church organization. He's Czech in heritage and not given to nonsense. He is also "designated lunch maker" in his household. "I was originally 'elected,' " he told me, "because I am the first riser and my wife doesn't function well in the morning. At first I didn't want to get up early. Who would? I grumbled."

But then Tom read the journals of Cotton Mather, an early American clergyman and writer who went about his day noticing God in the most mundane ways. (Mather even mentions how he contemplated his humanity before God while watching a dog relieve itself.) "I realized," Tom said, "I could pray my way through making the sandwiches and packing the lunch bags. I pray about the tests or presentations each person will face. It helps me claim the spiritual opportunity within the chore."

The daily becomes holy. A chore becomes charged with meanings barely dreamt of.

Some trace the word *religion* to the ancient roots *re* and *ligare*, suggesting the idea of retying. Religion in this sense does not mean untethering from life. The idea is to re-*fasten*, to re-*connect* to the Ground at the foundation of life. God leads us into the heart of things. The soul returns us to what we have forgotten or neglected. We re-*member* parts of life that seem cut off.

Such a view of spirituality helps me understand a perplexing passage in the Christian Bible written by Paul, a leader in the earliest church. He wrote letters to far-flung congregations in the ancient world, many of them comprised of servants and common workers. And to one congregation he said, "pray continually" ("pray without ceasing" in some translations). Did he expect them to forsake their daily lives, folding their legs under them, closing their eyes, never to return to the work world with its constant distractions? No; this is the same Paul who in a later letter chides hyperspiritual idlers who would not work. Such people he urged "to settle down and earn the bread they eat" (2 Thessalonians 3:12).

Paul knew that everyday life can be turned into a meeting ground. We already experience, every waking moment, the grist for praying. I do not simply squeeze more prayer into my schedule. I bring my life—work, play, sorrows—into my conversation with God. I come to see life and prayer as complementary, not competing. Our frustrations over our children, our disgust at constantly blowing our diet, our fear of illness and dying all *belong* in our spiritual life. Every day. If we see our lives as whole, we need not keep anything back.

I think of a man who, rushing from one thing to another, behind schedule, stubs his toe on the stairs. He blurts, "O God!" In an instant, the irony of his words begins to strike home. He realizes that he was reaching out, not with particularly reverent sentiments, but with "nonetheless a kind of prayer, groaning its way from the heart of my hassled, pressured self." *"Well,"* the harried man continues, *"if I'm praying, why not go all the way?"* So, on the next conscious breath, he breathes more deeply and repeats, "O God!" this time in a somewhat more friendly tone. And "on the third breath," he says, "I heard myself pray, with more feeling, 'O God . . . bless.' That one word, *bless,* evoked a cascade of feelings: *Bless my aching toe. Bless my ruffled spirits. Bless my frazzled body. Bless me in my heedless rush."*

The man concluded that he'd found a place to set up a practice of sustained, regular prayer: "right in the heartland of daily frustration itself."[9] Right where he was.

I know a man who communes with God while he mows his front grass. "While I push my lawn mower," Larry says, "I turn my mind toward God. I give thanks to God that I have the health to push a lawn mower. I notice the little things in my yard as I walk around. I see the neighborhood around me as I walk around in all directions. All these things inspire me to pray as I work—sometimes prayers of thanksgiving, sometimes prayers for the neighborhood children I see, sometimes prayers for the earth; the list goes on."

I want to do likewise, whatever my task. This morning, lying in bed, waiting for the day to begin, I found my mind rushing ahead to the day's events, to the people I was concerned about, the projects that loom over me. I also found myself able, at least at times, to turn my thoughts gently Godward. I made a subtle but essential shift.

Just as I did one Sunday not long ago. My family and I rushed to get ready and out the door to church on time. My wife was singing in the choir, leaving me to sit with and mind our five-year-old daughter. In our family's haste, Bekah had come to church partly undone—no one had put on the stretchy green decorative bands that covered her pony tails; these were important wardrobe elements to her and I had them in my pocket. We were seated as the opening music was sung, and by the time I got to Bekah's hair we had already come to the part of the worship service where the congregation reads aloud the psalm for the day. Bekah acted fidgety, and here I was, putting finishing touches on her hair while I could hear everyone around me reading the verses out loud. I could not hope to follow the reading. I wasn't even close to a mystic's exalted raptures. But as I worked on her, trying to avoid pulling her fine hairs, a phrase from the psalm being read aloud around me leapt out: "Show me your way, O Lord." Instantly, the Lord spoke through what I heard. God opened a way for me to pray. A harried moment became worship. I was met—and shaken from my distractedness, as I pray I will be again and again.

But there is more.

LET WAKING UP HAPPEN TO YOU
JUST AS YOU ARE

Part of us thinks, *Getting spiritually fit is fine for some people. But me? I'm not really that religious.* Perhaps some people along the way have aggravated the fear: a priest or aunt or neighbor. They leave the impression that spirituality belongs only to a hyperholy elite. Maybe they drop Latin phrases and mystify us with odd practices, making us afraid we won't have the jargon or the pedigree. We worry we won't be *good* enough or smart enough.

"I can't join the 'spiritually together' set," a woman confesses to a friend over a game of golf. "Some people are naturally attuned to God. Always have been. But not me." The woman's son has done drugs and rebelled. She feels terrible about herself and peeved at God. She goes to church—uncomfortably. Convinced she can't "win" at spirituality, she wonders, *With my past and at my age, why play the game?* Or a group of divorcées are talking about their struggles. "They felt themselves to be failures," writes Jesuit Gerard Hughes, "and considered it useless to try to pray, because they felt they had failed God as well as themselves and their partner." Religion only "intensified the pain, guilt, and sense of rejection. They felt alienated from God."[10]

But you don't have to be a saint to experience God in daily life. You don't have to invest sweat equity in impressing God. Someone once confessed to me with exasperation, "I try so hard at everything I do. I even bring an achievement orientation to my spiritual life." But the point is not spiritual accomplishments that we achieve as much as a grace we learn to receive. Granted, we don't greet God with a bored yawn. We are not passive in this. But neither must we think that cultivating the soul requires proven ability. We don't take on this as a massive self-improvement project. No, we let ourselves *be taken on* by a God more interested in us than we are in Him. Much of what happens when we pray comes from outside of us, from God's side. "You don't have to rush after it," Thomas Merton once wrote of the sacred. "It is there all the time. If you give it a chance it will make itself known to you."

In a big way, even our wanting comes from the times God draws close enough to awaken our heart's longing. Writes Howard Macy in *Rhythms of the Inner Life,* "God's initiating presence may be ever so subtle—an inward tug of desire, a more-than-coincidence meeting of words and events, a glimpse of the beyond in a storm or a flower—but it's enough to make the heart skip a beat and want to know more."[11] We are talking about an initiative prior to ours. A standing invitation. I'm not suggesting this process will become automatic or even easy. Just possible. For someone great and dependable assists us as we come.

So soon we find that whatever our feelings of spiritual inferiority (and we all wrestle with these), whatever our seemingly sorry track record (who's perfect?), whatever our defenses (we may even practice keeping God at a distance), becoming aware of God need not elude us. We never let where we start from disqualify us. Which means waking up spiritually may be simpler than you think. More than anything you learn to let down your guard and come. Because we cannot do everything does not mean we despair and do nothing. We learn to trust that God can work with what we have and are.

We also tell ourselves that much of our practice, especially at the beginning, will center around simple turns of the heart. So we take a few moments over lunch or before we hit the bed to invite God into our worlds. We do not worry about getting the words of our impromptu prayers just so. Or if I cannot spend an hour in the morning in prayer, I take ten minutes. If I cannot think about God every instant, I take a two-minute break mid-morning to breathe deeply and thank God for giving another day. And we take a similar approach to the people we try to love and live with.

I know a priest and monk, Father Eric, seventy-nine years old, full of joy. Once he went to Louisville, Kentucky, not far from his monastery, to hear the renowned worker with the poor, Mother Teresa of Calcutta, give a lecture. Afterward, Father Eric wrote her, told her how much he admired her work, and confessed that he did little to help the poor and needy.

Her reply was encouraging. "Do small things with great love," she wrote.

Those simple words led him to volunteer in the monastery's infirmary, helping to care for three monks who were dying. "It's not much," Father Eric told me, "but it's something I can do—and do with love."

Father Eric, also an accomplished calligrapher, took Mother Teresa's words and turned them into a simple poster, which now graces the wall near my phone, reminding me that the little matters more than I sometimes think. When it comes to the people I know or meet, I don't need always to perform heroically sacrificial acts. Little acts, done attentively, lovingly, change the world and carry the day.

And we don't have to accomplish everything this morning, or tomorrow, or next year. Any musician begins with scales and simple tunes. The poet has first to learn the alphabet like any other writer. Athletes start out with stretching. I find I pick up books now on prayer and spirituality that left me mystified years ago. I get at least glimmers of understanding. Things get better. Insights grow deeper. But the great secret is that God is with us from the beginning, even before we decide to "get spiritual." We can trust God to carry us along.

"Sometimes, noticing the moment," psychiatrist Gerald May writes, "I simply remember God. The remembrance does not take me out of the moment, because God is *in* the moment. It is what Brother Lawrence called the little interior glance, just a simple recognition of divine presence whenever immediate awareness happens."[12] Sometimes, May says, caught up in the day's stress, the best he can do is recall his desire to desire. His half-forgetful wanting becomes a kind of prayer in itself. But it is enough.

A story was told centuries ago to give pause to those who were proud of their spirituality and to encourage those who felt inadequate: A religious leader stood up in a grand sweep to pray in an ancient Hebrew temple, "God, I thank you that I am not like other men—robbers, evildoers, adulterers—or even like this tax collector." He recited a list of all he did "right": "I fast twice a week and give a tenth of all I get." Then you find out another man, a despised tax agent and governmental compromiser, was slinking in the shadows. He stood at a distance. "He would not even look up to heaven, but beat his breast and said, 'God, have mercy on me, a sinner.'" Jesus, who told the story, confounded his "righteous" hearers by concluding, "I tell you that this man, rather than the other, went home justified before God." And he gave hope to those who know they cannot get by without grace.

Some years ago my next-door neighbor's house caught fire late in the afternoon. Emily, I'll call her, hadn't made it home yet from her downtown Houston office. Another neighbor noticed the smoke and called the fire department. Not content simply to stand and watch a house burn, a couple of us began a frenzied attempt to hose the burning wall and roof of the garage. One neighbor found a sledgehammer and smashed a window on the garage door to allow us to hose water on the blaze at the back wall. We made an almost comical picture of motion and commotion.

Finally the fire trucks turned the corner into our cul-de-sac. In contrast to our nervous bustle and disorder, the firefighters arrived on the scene with measured calm. They donned protective garments and masks. They quietly unrolled their hoses. They peered into the garage's smoky blackness, determining the fire's location. Only when all was in place did they train their hoses on the flames and put out the fire.

When things settled down I mentioned the difference in approach to the fire chief supervising cleanup. "I would have rushed in with the hose," I said, "spraying everywhere."

"Well," he said, "you have to know what you are dealing with before you put out a fire. In a room like that the air reaches such temperatures that when you open the door and let oxygen in, it can all explode. Sometimes spraying water on a fire only drives it farther into a wall, or makes it spread in other directions. You cannot just rush in."

You cannot just rush in. I've thought about that many times. Rarely does frenetic activity do much good. Often my inflated sense of importance gets in the way of the everyday simple work of growing attentive to God, sensitive to others. I see that in my clearer moments. When letting your soul awaken, I believe, there is value in a gentle start. Some things should not be forced. You need not clamber in. It is not, after all, just a matter of our waking ourselves up, but also allowing a gentle Father to prod us to wakefulness. Wherever we find ourselves. Wherever God finds us.

Chapter 2

God

WITHIN REACH

You do not need to seek Him here or there, He is no further off than the door of your heart.
MEISTER ECKHART

Then I saw that the wall had never been there, that the "unheard-of" is here and this, not something and somewhere else.
DAG HAMMARSKJÖLD

Ten years ago I moved to a Chicago suburb to begin a new career, uprooting my wife and young children. I loved working for a magazine publisher, my first job in editing, but the four of us could afford only a cramped second-story apartment in a sprawling, crowded part of town. Money was tight. Our Ford sedan—the "blue bomb" we called it—threatened to expire at any time. We knew almost no one. One Saturday afternoon after a week that proved I had much to learn about my new job, I took a fitful nap. And I had an odd dream; I dreamt I was weeping.

It started when an old friend dropped by to talk. "I feel distant from God," she told me in the dream. I knew Joyce as a big-boned, middle-aged woman. A number of people—including me—came to her for guidance and unflappable certainty. But here she was, leaning her elbows on my dining room table, wondering, crying.

Then in my dream Joyce faded from view. I became the one who felt spiritually desolate. I picked up a theology book off the table, flipping through it—and wept. I turned to a newspaper article about God—and sobbed. Me, the writer and teacher on spirituality, and I blubbered at the mention of God. What a puzzling dream!

When my teenage son Micah recently overheard me telling the dream, he said, "I remember that, Dad. You didn't just dream you were crying, you really were. I heard you as you woke up and I came into your bedroom." He was so moved by the scene that he remembers it still, years later. And he recalled, as I hadn't, that my wife, Jill, came to my bedside to hold me and comfort me, a concerned look on her face.

The dream still intrigues *me*. Through it, I did more than cope with the normal anxieties of a move. I also came to grips with my intense need for God. *Could I turn to Him,* I wondered, *and know He would be there?*

Perhaps it's a question we all ask, in one way or another. We get too busy to think much about it, sometimes, too caught up or weighed down to wonder, but still we want to know: "Can an immeasurably good and powerful God help *me?*"

Even just the asking holds great promise. "One of the moral diseases we communicate to one another," writes the late Thomas Merton, "comes from huddling together in the pale light of an insufficient answer to a question we are afraid to ask."[1] But the right questions can help us wake up. They lead me out of myself to an encounter—with God, with others. They create a new openness. At times in my life when I have let God hover as a background fixture, when faith seemed no more than routine, I got by with a drowsy faith, without probing. But the deeper I go, the more I ask. And when need grows desperate, as it did when I moved to Chicago, the more the answers matter.

Now, years after my dream, I still find myself asking perhaps the most essential questions: *What is God really like? What difference will God make in how I live?* I want to know more about whom I come awake *to*. Here's what I tell myself as I ask:

THINK ABOUT SOMEONE BIG BEYOND IMAGINING, UNCONFINED BY CIRCUMSTANCES

I caught an early glimpse of the universe's sheer vastness when I was eight or so, riding in the backseat of our Chevrolet wagon on some country road in Southern California. We were all coming home from a day-long trip away from our suburban valley, where the nighttime glow of city lights always dimmed the stars. But lying in the backseat out in the back country, looking up at the pitch-black sky, I could see the Milky Way spattered in a vivid band that astonished and quieted me. Never had I seen it shine so bright. Never had I been so dazzled by the heavens. How much I connected that starry panorama to God, I don't know. But what I saw conditioned me to wider realities.

If you were to write my spiritual biography, you could string together the scenes of my life on the theme of my discovery that God was, time after time, bigger and better than I thought. I was cradled in the Methodist Church, one of what many call the main-line denominations. In the several churches of my childhood, Sunday morning worship was ordered, respectable. I learned about the Bible and living responsibly. Holidays were more than hollow forms. A simple prayer at family meals was a household fixture. But somehow I missed catching a bracing picture of God's grandeur. The sacred gently complemented, but rarely confounded our little worlds. But I remember one minister who came to our church not long before I moved away for grad school. We may live in a time, he said, more characterized by "Blah" than "Ah!" but it doesn't have to be so. I had already been growing hungry for more than an innocuous presence. Reverend Shelby spoke of a God who could not be contained.

I also fell in with the "Jesus People" movement in the early seventies, when I was in high school; amid the long hair, folk-rock worship music, and other trappings of Southern California culture I found a bracing faith. Here were people who believed big things about God, at times uncritically, but always fervently, exuberantly. As I went on to college and majored in religion, my categories got stretched again, this time intellectually and in terms of my social conscience. I gave up some unschooled assumptions, but the faith stayed alive, solid.

Or there was the time, years later, when God again loomed larger. This time it was great need that opened my eyes. I came home from New Jersey for a difficult summer break from grad school. That winter I had fallen for Jill, a fellow student at Princeton Seminary. We soon knew we wanted to marry. I tried, sometimes tearfully, to convince my parents to meet Jill. They thought I was too young at twenty-one, unready to take on marriage responsibilities.

During that tense summer, I got out of the house frequently, walking the sandy Santa Monica beaches near our home. The Pacific Ocean stretched past the western horizon, far beyond anything I could see. An expanse of sky spread out above me with an occasional seagull soaring and cawing. And there I felt surrounded by a vast, comforting reality. I realized my life played out under a power not bound by my immediate dilemmas and pain. I came back to the house able to go on.

The widening of the categories has happened again and again. In the eighties, charismatic renewal, a movement of Christians known for their lively worship and interest in healing and other manifestations of the miraculous, drew my attention and in a way drew me in. My Princeton-trained mind was intrigued by phenomena I had not observed in the classroom. One afternoon—I was by now a pastor—I was visiting church members who were recovering from surgery. I began praying, right in the car, much as I had hundreds of times before. Only this time I felt God sweep through my fumbling words. My habitual prayers were given an electric intensity. From within myself—and yet beyond myself—poured forth an energy I could not have manufactured on my own, a speaking in unknown tongues. That weekend I went for a walk near the wooded creek in the back of our Virginia house. The woods were hushed. Snow gently fell and coated tree limbs and stones in soft white. And a warm and prayerful gratefulness gathered and arose from within. I felt as though I was being *prayed through*. It was another awakening.

Around this time my wife asked for a book for her birthday: the autobiography of Thomas Merton, *The Seven Storey Mountain*. "To Jill," I inscribed it; "May this year ahead be full of unfolding discoveries and vital faith, for you, for us." When Jill was done reading, I started Merton's book and put it down in frustration, mystified about all the fuss over it. A few months later I picked it up again and read it through. And this time I found myself awed by his discovery of God—his passion for encounter with the One who, he would later write in *No Man Is an Island*, makes seekers "leave their own ideas and their own words behind them." What I read changed me. And led me to yet other rediscoveries: the classical spiritual writings of Augustine, Teresa of Avila, Evelyn Underhill, Oswald Chambers—writers from varied cultures and eras who, like Merton, fed my longing to meet a God who intervenes, overturns, transforms. They still keep me watching, keep me from limiting God.

And now, sometimes when I least expect it, there are those times I sit in a worship service and somehow see a larger backdrop of cosmic significance. Episcopalian that I now am, the prayers I hear go back centuries, some of them. I listen as my minister prays, "We praise you, joining our voices with angels and archangels and with all the company of heaven. . . ." Then the whole congregation sings an ancient hymn that begins, "Holy, holy, holy, Lord, God of power and might, heaven and earth are full of your glory." I sometimes have a fleeting sense of the heavenly throngs, out of sight but not far from imagination, surrounding the ineffable Presence at the heart of creation.

We inhabit a universe where, I'm told, to hold out a dime at arm's length would block fifteen million stars, if our eyes could see with that power. The bigness boggles our minds. But it's more than sheer size that amazes. It is the Creator of this grand sweep, the hand behind the handiwork, who awes us. Unseen glories that are just hinted at by the ones we catch with our eyes. "After the one extravagant gesture of creation," writes poet and essayist Annie Dillard, "the universe has continued to deal in extravagances."[2] I walk around, drive to work, pull up the covers on a sleep-in Saturday morning under titanic mysteries that shape my minuscule life—and yours. Beyond the world of rocks and tables and hamburgers and stars another realm carries on. The God of all things infiltrates life, making every moment rife with unfathomed power. I barely notice, and usually only glimpse these things, but a wonderfully adequate God, a host of angels, and an infinite heavenly spaciousness fill the universe in which we live.

John Franklin, best man at my wedding and something of a soul friend, speaks of how it was with him:

> I was a second-year student at Auckland University [in New Zealand], with a great longing within me that none of my conventional Sunday religion seemed to touch. One morning, when I probably should have been in the library, I lay under a tree on the university grounds, looking up at the blue sky through the green leaves. I felt myself filled with a sense of wonder. I found myself praying something to the effect of, "You have to be bigger than what they say about you! I want to know you. Show me who you are." At the same time, I was idly fanning with a thumb the pages of a little New Testament and Psalms book I had with me. The pages were rifling quickly, but a bug flew in. Rather than squash it into the page, I stopped. I was about to brush it off when I saw it sitting on these words from Psalm 66:20: "Blessed be God, because he has not rejected my prayer or removed his steadfast

love from me!" Well, blessed be the bug! This was
a turning point. It was God I wanted most. And
God was with me, using his servant the bug to
communicate something. The experience left no doubt
in me that God heard my longing. This seemed so
much more real, so much bigger than anything talked
about in church. Then followed the awesome journey
of discovering that God would fill my life with
nothing less than God's very self.

Such intimations come in all kinds of ways. Once God asked a
man named Job, hurting, tired, unable to imagine much beyond his
own daily grind,

> *Can you bind the beautiful Pleiades?*
> *Can you loose the cords of Orion?*
> *Can you bring forth the constellations in their seasons*
> *or lead out the Bear with its cubs?*
> *Do you know the laws of the heavens?*
> *Can you set up God's dominion over the earth? (Job 38:31–32).*

They were rhetorical questions, of course, pointedly asked.
But they would eventually help lift Job out of his distress. They
spoke of secret, vast immensities, no small encouragement when it
seems that not much is happening or ever will happen. But a big
God replenishes our capacity to be astonished. We find ourselves
looking outward, heavenward, pondering mysteries that maybe we
thought we didn't have time for, but that we realize we cannot live
without. We see the vastness as more than a curiosity for a scientist,
but an invitation for a worshiper. And they remind us of sacred

wonders in a way that opens possibilities for our lives. Our understanding of business as usual is stretched wide open.

Not long ago I was driving home from my office at the religious publisher where I worked part-time. It had been a productive, satisfying day, but I felt drained. I had little energy to think about becoming more spiritually "attuned." I wondered, *How can spirituality help me now?*

The question helped me slowly to turn my thoughts to God. It seemed that even just calling Him to mind opened me to resources beyond the limits and littleness of my circumstances. Before I knew it, my questioning became an encounter with the One who could bring precisely what I needed to carry on. God brought renewing power. I felt better, stronger, just knowing He existed. My fatigue dissolved into a time of refreshment. It was another little awakening.

The next day I was sitting in my living room, reading the Psalms. I came across a verse that was a prayer: "O my strength, I watch for you" (Psalm 59:9). I tried to make the prayer my own, saying it several times, slowly, thoughtfully. And I tried to recall it through the day, tried to watch for God, asking, "What do you want to do? How can your strength help me?" I opened myself to the source of life and power.

There is an unsettling side to this, of course. Talk of a God who cannot be contained by our thoughts takes us beyond the familiar. A part of us wants to whittle God down to our size, turn Him into something we think we can handle. Junk soul food and "spirituality lite" offer a certain appeal. I mean, it's one thing to get in touch with our "spiritual selves," but turning heart and soul to the phenomenal glories of an infinite God? No wonder Augustine once exclaimed to God, "Your light shone upon me in its brilliance, and I thrilled with love and dread alike." We hesitate, resort to diversionary tactics, pare God down. Lately, a friend of mine said, "I've learned that I had God in a box—one of my own making." We prefer the comforts of a household deity we can own and possess.

But only sometimes. In our deepest selves we know that "Nothing less than God is sufficient for us," as the medieval English hermit Julian of Norwich wrote. We don't really want to tame God. A small God, I once heard someone say, is small hope. Nothing less than the matchless, majestic God will inspire us. "The house of my soul is too small for you to come to it," prayed Augustine. "May it be enlarged by you."[3] May it be so, I pray. For I remember that, in the words of a Hebrew prophet millennia ago, God's ways are higher than our ways and His thoughts than our thoughts, just as the infinite skies are higher than the earth.

I have heard of a prayer that says only, "Wonderful, Wonderful, Wonderful." Sometimes my response to the greatness of God does not reduce easily to words. I turn, after all, to One whom an ancient biblical writer said "alone is immortal and who lives in unapproachable light, whom no one has seen or can see." To this God, the verse concludes, "be honor and might forever." And so I keep my eyes open to that which is beyond comprehension.

OPEN YOURSELF TO SOMEONE WHO DRAWS CLOSE, LETTING NOTHING COME BETWEEN

My wife is out of town, visiting her elderly mother. She has been gone for days and I miss her. Actually, I ache for her. Something deep within me makes it difficult for me to wait till she comes home.

Our phone calls help a bit. But not for long. Not really. I long for her embrace. I can hardly wait to look into her eyes. I want her *here*.

I think the longing for God, when we don't cover it up, is similar:

> *As the deer pants for streams of water,*
> *so my soul pants for you, O God.*
> *My soul thirsts for God, for the living God.*
> *When can I go and meet with God?*
> *My tears have been my food*
> *day and night,*
> *while men say to me all day long,*
> *"Where is your God?" (Psalms 42:1–3)*

What we hunger for is not so much belief, then, but presence. Not a concept but a Companion. Someone who walks beside us. A God as close as our selves, as life-giving as our breath.

To be impressed by God's immensity helps wake me up. But on a deep level I long to know, does the unsearchable become accessible? Sometimes the sublime God of our imaginations seems far removed from the stresses of sales reports or worries about an ailing uncle. "The biggest problem," I once heard someone say, "is feeling sometimes like I don't connect." But if God would immerse Himself in my daily life by coming close, *that* would be different. That would catch just about anyone's attention. So we need to find out if God is really *here*.

A couple of centuries ago, around the time of the American Revolution, a philosophy known as Deism answered the question in a rather austere way. Deists pictured God as a watchmaker who created the universe, wound it up, set it running, and stepped back. The created order was self-sufficient, in a way. It required no further involvement or investment from above. God drew back from any involvement in our daily affairs—we were mere humans—and took a vacation of sorts.

But there is another way of looking at God: as a being who not only creates, but also sustains. Who will not absent Himself from the creatures into whom He tenderly breathed life. Who, in the words of the fourteenth-century mystic Julian of Norwich, shows Himself maker and lover and *keeper* of all that is. Who enters the world—and our lives.

On a recent Christmas Eve, surrounded by candlelight and festive altars decked in greens, I joined in singing the old carol, "O Come, All Ye Faithful." One snatch of a verse struck me, a prayer to the Son whose birth we were making so much of that night: "You abhorred not the virgin's womb." A strange, poetical image. At first I even missed what it was saying. Then it hit me: God did not shrink from joining His life to ours. In the person of Jesus, He was willing to walk our dusty roads, sweat through the things that worry us. Even die. "In a town called Bethlehem," writes Frederick Buechner, "a child was born who, beyond the power of anyone to account for, was the high and lofty One made low and helpless. . . . The one whom none can look on and live is delivered in a stable under the soft, indifferent gaze of cattle."[4] So willing was God to involve Himself that He subjected Himself to my everyday, sometimes comical limits. He became accessible, vulnerable. Someone I can relate to, even now. Someone I can miss when in my busyness I forget to notice or when in my pain He seems far away. Someone who yet comes. This, the Bible tells me, is the nature of God.

Just today I was helping my fifteen-year-old son with his high school literature class. He's reading Shakespeare's *Romeo and Juliet* (and barely able to stomach all the mushy sentiment). I tried to help Micah appreciate it. And I was struck by the scene in which Juliet, hidden in the night's darkness, realizes Romeo stands below her window, out in the garden. Both know that their families have nursed a deadly feud. Romeo risked all to come; his discovery would mean certain death. When she realizes he is there, she asks how he came. Why did he not stay away? His answer:

> *With love's light wings did I [fly over] these walls,*
> *For stony limits cannot hold love out,*
> *And what love can do, that dares love attempt. . . .*[5]

When first I read that, I saw it as a kind of parable of our passionate search for God. Our willingness to dare whatever our hunger for God asks of us. But the more I think about it now, it makes an even better picture of God's refusal to hold Himself aloof from those whom He has made. God does not stand back. No fence keeps Him out. No circumstance in my life need separate me from His presence. Even with our walls high and impenetrable, God dares to come near.

For three years I studied theology at Princeton Theological Seminary, next door to the prestigious university of the same name. Amid ivied stone buildings, I learned about Augustine, Calvin, and the Anabaptists. I nailed the pronunciation of theologians with daunting German names. I mastered plans for running smooth church programs. My cognitive knowledge grew by synaptic leaps. But at times I wanted to do more than make God the object of term papers and test-taking. I needed more than professional competence.

My restlessness drove me to other students—John, Maclain, Sherry—who also hungered for more. I can't remember who came up with the idea, but we met for daily prayer at the school's chapel at 6:30—A.M.! Why? This was not likely to help anyone's grades. The prayers we offered were simple, heartfelt, and mostly spontaneous—no experiments in liturgical innovation. Why wake up before dawn and stumble to a cold chapel? We wanted to become more alert and spiritually alive. We felt something attracting us, something that on a deep level we sensed could transfigure our lives and work. We gathered in expectation of an encounter, not only with one another but with a palpable Presence. A Someone there, ready to come *here*.

I know a monk who lived in a strict religious order for twenty-five years. He fasted. He gave up normal human relationships. He spent seven of those years in a cabin as a consecrated hermit. He so longed to meet God that he forsook everything. He would spend hours and hours each day seeking God. He felt driven by his longing.

One morning as he prayed, it seemed God said to him, inaudibly but nevertheless powerfully, that the Presence he had been so fervently seeking he possessed: "You already live in it." William eventually left his monastery, became a missionary to Bolivia, and married. Now an Episcopal priest, he has rejoined the world of everyday life, of changing diapers and making supper and fighting traffic. And God is every bit as real. You can hear it in his strong, resonant voice. "I had thought I was connecting with God only when I prayed, or worshiped, or somehow consciously thought about God," he told me. But God was already there, waiting. Close.

In my own ways, in my own situations, I want to live with more awareness of that which is already there. Some days I feel out of practice, or like a tourist traversing new territory. I sometimes have trouble enough slowing down to catch my breath, much less to ponder the nearness of God. But the way is simple. "You do not need to seek [God] here or there," writes Meister Eckhart, "He is no further than the door of your heart."[6] So I watch. Stay open. I try to avoid thinking I amass rules and disciplines to make God "show up." I tell myself to wait with the assurance that God will allow nothing to separate the soul that seeks Him.

We will know times, of course, when we don't feel much. This can distress anyone. Let it come as no surprise, this "dark night of the soul," as John of the Cross called it in the sixteenth century. But it need not throw us off. Even God's absence points, in a way, to His reality. That I don't always feel God does not prove God does not exist or draw close. On the contrary, in a way it suggests the opposite. My missing God, as I did in my dream during that fitful Saturday nap soon after my move to Illinois, points to a God whose very absence reminds of a sweet presence.

I have known people who say that when a loved one dies they feel the reality of that person's life all the more. We notice a friend's not taking a walk with us precisely because we normally *have* someone whose presence we enjoy. We feel an awkward pause in conversation with a group of friends at a party because there had just been animated discussion and laughter. It is that way with our awareness of God.

Spiritually waking up will not mean I never miss God. But God's nearness leads me to experience those absences differently, more hopefully. I will notice the seeming distance as a longing, as a sensation that places in me a more urgent yearning. The emptiness becomes a prelude for experiencing the One we long for; the One we sense in our inner selves can be wonderfully, gladly met.

But there is yet more I tell myself when thinking about God.

PICTURE SOMEONE WHO LOVES MORE THAN YOU CAN KNOW, ANSWERING YOUR DEEPEST LONGING

Once, in the stale, cigarette smoke–filled air of a very ordinary restaurant, I heard words that matter wonderfully to a son. My father blessed my marriage. My parents' early disapproval seemed forgotten. It reminded me of the times when I was in high school and college and Dad ascended the creaking stairs to my room after I had turned off the light. "How was your day?" he'd ask. And in the quiet shadows and breezes of my room in that Santa Monica home he'd tell me he was proud. I felt accepted.

That Sunday afternoon at a Denny's restaurant, as we waited for a table—he and Mom, myself and my wife and children—he quietly said, "I'm proud of you. You have great kids, a good wife— you're doing well." That is what I choose to remember. That is also what I need to hear God tell me.

When we are grieving or stressed out we may give audience to the tired voices that tell us we aren't worth much to God, that God doesn't like us or notice us. John Mulholland, a man I've met on the Internet, recently wrote, "I grew up with a view of God who was pinch-faced, more interested in condemning as many as possible than loving all his creatures. This view was tinged with just enough of the loving God that I did not rebel immediately, but I did so eventually and I now know that if I had a true image of our Awesome God I would not have needed to."

Growing up, I avoided the judgmentalism of John's childhood church experience. From a young age I repeatedly heard Bible verses like "God so loved the world that he gave his only Son." But much of what I have felt inside belied that assurance. I know in my head that God would not neglect me, harm me. But still I live as if I haven't really woken up to the reality of it. I berate myself internally for mistakes. Or feel chronic guilt over things I did that I shouldn't have. Or feel bad about things I didn't do that I should have. Much of the time I have not felt much at all, at least not like a beloved child. I am like Kevin, who admits, "All those years I secretly feared God didn't accept me the way I was." So I worry. Most of us are our own worst critics.

And we grow afraid. Perhaps if we were truly known, we fear, we will be found lacking. We worry that the worst things we have done will be with us forever. And we transfer that to our relationship with God. He stands over us as Judge and naysayer, we fear, ready to make our coming humiliating and taxing, "always snooping around," as someone wrote, "after sinners." We picture a celestial policeman, a strict moral scorekeeper.

Waking up requires another picture of God. Nothing has done more to draw me to God than the conviction that God overflows with compassion beyond measure, that God is "mercy upon mercy upon mercy," as one writer put it. The God known as the awesome

God of power and might cares enough to hold my hand. Nothing can awaken a soul like love.

But how easily I forget that I am loved. Many people—parents, teachers, aunts, friends, a brother—have loved me. I have been praised for success. Loved by a wife and children. But I am like my friend Chris de Vinck. "I repeat prayers," he confesses, "that have more to do with ritual than they have to do with the hand of my father stroking my cheek when I was ten." I remain unconvinced too often.

I need constant reminders. I learn from Mary Lee, a gray-haired pray-er and fervent believer. She comes out of a "performance-oriented background," she told me. Everyone in her household aimed for perfection. "Giving ninety percent—to anything—wasn't good enough. You always did your very best. But I often felt like I didn't measure up. And somewhere I picked up in my thinking that God was always watching, waiting for me to make a mistake so He could hit me over the head." Then a friend gave her a paper on which someone had typed twenty-three attributes of God. On the list was God's power, His ability to know all things, His willingness to be always present. But what really caught Mary Lee was its description of God's love: "God so loves that He gives Himself for another, even to the laying down of His own life. He desires the other's highest good without any thought for Himself."

Testimonies from the wisest of spiritual counselors, those who have gone the way ahead of us, tell us that the picture is better than we can hope or imagine. God, whom we may sometimes fear or paint as distant or aloof, turns out to be *good*. Because of His grace our failings turn out not to be the obstacles we feared. "It seems to me," writes Thomas Merton, "the most absurd thing in the world to be upset because I am weak and distracted and blind and constantly make mistakes! What else do I expect! Does God love me any less because I can't make myself a saint by my own power and in my own way?"[7]

God loves. God personifies love. God *is* love, writes John in the New Testament. If, by Jesus' coming, God demonstrated His willingness to be involved in human life, by Jesus' death, God goes further to prove His saving love. He turns the chasm of our alienation into a bridge. The sacrificial death of Jesus on the cross becomes our salvation. "How wonderful and beyond our knowing," I read in *The Book of Common Prayer*, "is your mercy and loving-kindness to us, that to redeem a slave, you gave us a son."[8] Such a God of goodness will not obliterate us. We turn to God to receive a love freely, gladly offered.

Does it sound too good to be true? Is there really no catch? We have trouble receiving pure mercy. We try to ensure that we present ourselves spruced up. We think we can "help" God in the mercy department. But we end up getting in the way.

Not long ago I took Bekah, six at the time, for an audition for a production of *The Wizard of Oz,* sponsored by a local school and a traveling children's theater. All along she just assumed that she would get a part; she wanted to be a munchkin, and the thought that she might not seemed never to occur to her. I encouraged her, but didn't say anything about her chances. I certainly didn't want to undermine her confidence and suggest she might not get in.

But then I had no idea that 250 children would show up for the fifty available parts. In a huge gymnasium, the two directors had the children line themselves around the four edges of the cavernous building, the tallest on one end trailing down to the shortest on the other end. Bekah, in with high schoolers and junior highers, stood near the end of the building. The directors went through the line, having each child say his or her name and age. Then they did it again, this time urging, "Say your name *loud*. Say it with animation." The boisterous, enthusiastic kids were told to sit down, marking them in a kind of first cut. I watched as they finally got to Bekah. I was at the opposite end, but my heart sank when I could not hear her. She was too quiet, too restrained.

The directors gave the kids other chances, other quick assignments. But I could never hear Bekah. I knew she was not standing out. It was the expressive, outgoing kids who were getting the parts, I could tell.

Finally the long two hours came to a close with the kids all gathered in a knot around the directors. The names of the chosen fifty were read off a list. I knew already Bekah hadn't made it. She didn't know it till she heard the last name read.

Bekah threaded her way to me, cheeks flushed, through crowds of people leaving. She hugged me hard as we prepared to walk out. "I'm proud of you," I said. "I am so impressed that you auditioned." Then I said, quietly, "I'm sorry you didn't get a part."

That broke Bekah's tear floodgates. She grabbed at me and sobbed. I picked her up and she buried her face in my shoulder. She could not stop crying.

I tried to comfort her. As I carried her to the door of the girls' bathroom, she began to relax a little. I promised to take her out to Red Lobster for supper. We went, and it was a poignant, precious time.

The next morning, I overheard Bekah talking with her mother.

"The kids who got parts didn't behave right," she said. "*I* was good. I was quiet like I was supposed to be. And I didn't get a part!" Then it hit me: She had equated goodness with restraint. She was trying hard, but in the wrong way. She thought the directors wanted reserve, stiff attention, frozen alertness. That was "good." But Bekah didn't understand: The directors wanted energy, emotion, *loudness.* They wanted kids who could be themselves with abandon. Who might go too far in recklessness, but nevertheless showed energy. Bekah had tried so hard to be good that it froze her personality.

Many people, I suspect, feel that way around God. As if they can't relax and simply receive God's wondrous grace. Someone I know tells of growing up in a church where "it seemed like most of the folks were always frowning. I seriously thought my dad wouldn't fit in there even if he miraculously decided to come some Sunday because he didn't frown enough." So we end up rigid, tight. And we miss an opportunity to be ourselves, to awaken, as we are, to the grace-filled kindness of God.

I never had another dream like the one I recounted earlier from the beginning of my editing career. At least that I remember. But I recall another picture of God, just as vivid. It came from my wife, who was not dreaming, but praying. Suddenly an image of God appeared in her mind. "God was holding His hands out, palms open," Jill said, "waiting for me to place my hands in His. He was just waiting for me to come." I like that picture.

"Do not imagine," writes one wise spiritual teacher, "that God is like a carpenter who works or not, just as he pleases, suiting his own convenience. It is not so with God, for when He finds you ready He must act, and pour into you, just as when the air is clear and pure the sun must pour into it. . . . Surely, it would be a very great defect in God if He did not do a great work, and anoint you with great good, once He found you empty and innocent."[9]

At the heart of the universe is a God who calls me—constantly—to make Him a part of life. I make room best by remembering this invitation. By realizing that God can be trusted. By letting God come and make me new.

Chapter 3

Ways
WE WAKE

The world
will never starve for wonders
but only for the want of wonder.
G. K. CHESTERTON

In November 1983, as a twenty-eight-year-old man, I returned to my childhood Santa Monica home with a new set of eyes.

When I had left in the summer of 1977, I planned, over my parents' protests, to marry. My proceeding with the wedding opened a rift in our relationship that took years to mend. It would be six years until I came home again. Thousands of miles between us, my parents' ailing health, and my tight finances all conspired against a reunion, even when the birth of Abram, their first grandchild, thawed the relationship.

A business trip Jill and I planned for Thanksgiving week finally brought about my homecoming. We were attending a conference not far from my family's Santa Monica home. It was the perfect occasion to gather—this time with Jill and the boys, making it a true family Thanksgiving. Memories flooded me from the moment we walked up the steps of their pastel sea-green stucco house perched on a rise above the sidewalk. My eyes took in the familiar worn places in the gold shag carpet, the tropical flowers in the backyard, the view of the Pacific from what had been my second-story bedroom. I showed my boys the park along the coastal palisades, a couple of blocks away, where growing up I had spent hours walking and jogging. I was seeing everything afresh.

Most of all, I took in my parents' faces. During a spare moment of our stay, I pulled out my journal and wrote, "I feel great love for my parents when I look into their eyes. And I feel it from them." I had been nervous before coming, but now I relaxed and felt grateful. And I really *saw* them, felt their presence. I don't think I casually noticed anything that trip. I walked through my old haunts with heightened sensitivity. I wanted to absorb it all.

If you are like me, events and experiences often roll over you, until something, like a separation or illness, yanks you from your distracted, half-tied ways of noticing. Frequently, I do not make the pieces of my life fully my own. I run from here to there on automatic pilot. I don't take in the draping folds of a dining room tablecloth, the Christmas tree lights blinking softly on the tree, the contours and lines of a beloved's hand. Or I greet someone, asking how things are going, and then I fail to look into her eyes to read the subtler signals that convey the real answer. "Immediate awareness is killed in countless ways," writes psychiatrist Gerald May, "in work, in play, in human relationships, in food, in worry, in racing toward success. It is no accident that one says 'I lost myself,' to describe the drowning of awareness in activity. . . . We awaken to immediate living only now and then."[1]

But there's hope. We can learn to be more fully present. It involves a process. But it begins now. Indeed we have, just by growing up, already begun in a way. "I woke in bits, like all children," writes Annie Dillard, "piecemeal over the years. I discovered myself and the world, and forgot them, and discovered them again."[2] Parts of us wake up in odd moments. We notice things in sharper relief, or see things that, for all we had known, weren't there. We understand what we once had no clue about. We no longer feel as if we sleepwalk through the scenes of our lives.

The coming awake may happen with the place we live. Instead of the stained carpet, the dusty coffee table, the creaking kitchen floor, we look around and say, "This is *home.*" Or it happens with our children. Suddenly, after days of tolerating them, we wake up to how much we cherish them. We see them not as interruptions in our schedules, not all the time, at least, but as gifts from God. Maybe the awareness comes at our workplace, where we have complained and schemed to leave; suddenly we feel grateful to work, to share tasks with colleagues, to be able to pay the mortgage. Even Monday mornings don't seem so bad. Or our prayer times seem flat, unpromising, godforsaken. Then, often for reasons we cannot trace, we sense God's touch. We wake up in the mornings and want eagerly to pray.

How do we make ourselves ready for such moments?

Simple things do it. A childlikeness serves us well here. Children naturally live with immediacy. Once Jesus called a little child and had him stand among those he was teaching. And he said: "I tell you the truth, unless you change and become like little children, you will never enter the kingdom of heaven" (Matthew 18:2–3). So how to recover an unstrained alertness? How do we, bit by bit, become more aware?

Here is what I know.

LISTEN TO WHAT YOUR LIFE IS
ALREADY TELLING YOU

In a bookstore one October day over a dozen years ago, I stumbled on to something that would change the way I think about my life. My wife had noticed a wire rack of titleless books with gold foil-embossed covers. I opened one up, finding nothing inside but blank pages. The idea was to use the book to keep a diary or record recipes or sketch drawings. As we browsed, I remember my wife suggesting, offhandedly, "You should start keeping a journal. It might help you in writing sermons. And besides, it would be something to pass down to the children and grandchildren." I was a pastor at the time, and it seemed like good advice. "Hmm," I think I said. With little discussion, we each bought a blank book. I thought of it only as an experiment. Soon, however, I was writing a page or two every few days, logging stirrings I noticed or events I wanted to remember. I wrote about interesting people in the church I was working at, about awaking in the night with our newborn son, about dreams for my future. Questions about vocation filled many of my entries, as a later chapter will show.

I have kept at it ever since. I rarely am disciplined about it, sometimes going weeks without an entry. But something always draws me back. I believe I write, however erratically, because I want to relish the scraps and milestones, to hold some of them close to my ear, as I used to do with conch shells to hear of the sounds of the beach's waves. Sometimes the clarity and true import comes only months, even years, after the experiencing and writing. Every now and then I pull an old volume off the shelf, just to see where I've been, and what it means for where I'm going. Writing it down, reading it later, helps me not forget.

Keeping a journal is not the only way to listen to a life, of course. Writing a newsy letter, telling a loved one a special memory, taking a class in writing your spiritual autobiography can carry similar benefits, not just to others, but to us. Something as simple as pausing at the end of the day helps us hear events' deeper meanings. The point is to pay attention to what life would tell us, if only we listen. Every day contains clues and hints that help orient us if we don't forget to let them find us.

In our chatty, noisy world, listening to our lives is not always easy. And it's not just the sheer volume of honking cars or booming radios. I get distracted by subtler voices: Ads that constantly urge me to be this or buy that. Movies that dazzle but leave me with confusing messages. A seemingly endless stack of papers and books that vie for attention. Even loved ones who would verbally press me into their molds. My mental habits get conditioned by a culture that often runs at cross purposes to spiritual wakefulness. The many words dull my hearing. I forget to attend to a still, small voice amid the agitating torrent of sound.

Even when we pray it may seem little better. Our souls resemble noisy rooms full of many voices. Wake up in the morning, C. S. Lewis, once wrote, and "all your wishes and hopes for the day rush at you like wild animals."[3] I know what he means. I must make a concerted effort to listen. I have to create quiet spaces where a sound other than my own agenda and gabby wonderings can resonate.

But through life's daily noise does come that larger voice. It speaks and beckons and invites our attention. In an old Mel Brooks routine, the psychiatrist tells his patient, "Listen to your broccoli, and it will tell you how to eat it." For all the silliness of that scene, it gives us a truth about waking up spiritually. Somehow we begin to push aside the bustling activities, the demands of others, the incessant drive to accomplish. And we find ourselves able to open our ears. "Put the ear of my heart next to your lips," prayed Augustine.

One of my favorite Bible passages suggests a practical way to do this. When, in biblical times, the Lord began calling a young Hebrew boy named Samuel to be a prophet, he did not realize it was God's voice. Samuel ran to his guardian, Eli, the temple priest. Samuel thought he had heard Eli's voice in the first place. But Eli knew better, knew it was a larger Voice. The old priest told the puzzled youth, "Go and lie down, and if [God] calls you, say, 'Speak, Lord, for your servant is listening'" (1 Samuel 3:9). Samuel did, and the Lord spoke. Sometimes I take Samuel's prayer and repeat it gently, making it my own. I use it to cultivate a listening attitude.

These days, people bold enough to claim that God is speaking to them may be referred to therapy. But God does speak. And God often begins with the circumstances and turns of our lives. We shouldn't dismiss even seemingly insignificant occurrences, not if we live through them reverently. We scan for deeper meanings and hidden connections. When the inner chatter quiets, we hear surprising, stretching things about who we are—and *why* we are. We find a way, somehow, to listen to what God may be trying to tell us.

I think of the old way of describing a story's plot: You don't simply say, "The king died. The queen died." These two sentences are nothing more than bare statements. You have a plot only when you connect the events: "The king died and then the queen died *of grief.*" We find in any good story something that weaves the separate events into a whole. So it is with our lives. A great interweaving Presence, working in and through what we do and experience, carries forward purposes we at first get only glimmers of. Writes my friend Christopher de Vinck, "In many ways we are like the lost Alice in Wonderland, being stretched and pulled in different directions as we travel through the dark tunnels of life, but then we see a hint of order, a sense of who we are."[4]

Maybe it's a book we stumble across at the library that changes our view of things. A doctor who frowns over a suspicious X-ray, who later figures out what it will take to make us well. The personnel director of one company who says, "Maybe we'll call you back," while another asks, "When can you start?" One romance sputters and dies, while another leads to a wedding aisle. Much of what happens to us appears, at least on the surface, to intersect our lives routinely or by accident. And yet, looking back, we see a plot unfolding. Who could know that the young woman I met at a grad school student orientation retreat at Atlantic City, New Jersey, two years later would become my wife and in time the mother of my three children? Out of the dozens of people I met that weekend, her face, her smile, her name, would unalterably change my life. Coincidence? No. In the many turns and surprises, it is, Evelyn Underhill writes, "as if a hidden directive power, personal, living, free, were working through circumstances."[5] This is no impersonal fate, but signs of an Author who can shape a story line in ways we can only glimpse, that we cooperate with through a willing heart. Writes Frederick Buechner, "Deep within history as it gets itself written down in history books and newspapers, in the letters we write and in the diaries we keep, is sacred history, is God's purpose working itself out in the apparent purposelessness of human history and of our separate histories."[6]

And we know that God has already done much to speak, to meet our listening ears with what we need to hear. He has given us a revealed purpose in Scripture, for example, that helps us place our little story in the context of God's larger story. We don't figure this all out for ourselves, flailing in the dark. I remember when I started pulling a Bible off my bedroom bookshelf. I had been given the Bible as a child, but rarely opened it. I felt driven to read by spiritual curiosity more than anything, by a vague sense that I didn't really know what lay between the covers of the book that so many said was important. For who knows what reason, there in my bedroom those afternoons after school, something clicked as I read the stories of Jesus. And in the days that followed, what had been quaint stories and dry history ushered me into a living encounter. I met One who suddenly appeared to walk with me through my days. Why did it "take"? Why then? Who can say? I mainly paid attention, observed something growing within me that brought a quiet joy and profound warmth. I would awaken in the mornings, sunlight streaming in my room, galvanized with an urge to talk to God. I knew that Jesus had made it possible.

Much of listening, then, means heeding what God has already revealed. We have something against which the aberrations of our own spiritual eccentricities can be measured, corrected. We read and hear the Bible's words and stories not just for information, but for truth about God, Jesus, the Holy Spirit. Scripture is like a river, someone wrote, "broad and deep: shallow enough for a lamb to go wading, but deep enough for an elephant to go swimming."[7] We don't rush through our times in its pages, but ruminate. "Creative brooding," someone calls such reading. I try to approach other great writing the same way, absorbing the insights of holy people, the centuries' spiritual greats, whose lives have been formed by immersion in Scripture's truth and God's guidance.

And who knows, God may speak to us some afternoon, some anxious moment, some time of seeking and wondering. The other day, out for a morning run, I felt keen anxiety about my son's going off to college. And the expected source of income for his tuition had dried up. But I had the sense to do more than stew over it. I tried to listen. And in the space of quiet I felt God tell me to relax, utterly. God was giving a word of reassurance.

In all kinds of ways, through a book we read, a friend's phone call, a quiet insight, God says, "It's like this . . ." We hear a still, small voice, impressing a direction on our conscience, or even, wonder of wonders, speaking directly, as happened with young Samuel. I try to make times of simple listening a part of my prayer times because of that.

KEEP YOUR FOCUS ON THE HERE AND NOW

I recall elementary school, sitting in a classroom while the teacher took the roll. When my name was called out, I would answer, "Present," or "Here." It did not matter, at least at that point, if I was half-asleep or daydreaming about getting home to play with my friends or wondering what I was going to do when summer vacation rolled around. She needed to know only if I had shown up. If I had, if the others had, the day's tasks could begin. She had something to work with.

Once a well-known author was asked how to become a writer. The questioner had romantic visions, I suppose, of the writing life. But the author's answer would have pleased my grade-school teacher. He simply said, "Buy a table and chair, get a pad of paper and a pen, and then *be there.*" When inspiration comes, you can't be someplace else.

Only when we allow ourselves to be present to our circumstances can we hope to wake up spiritually. The present is the raw material we have to work with. It is where we have possibilities to grasp. "How we spend our days is, of course, how we spend our lives," writes Annie Dillard. "What we do with this hour, and that one, is what we are doing."[8] So part of waking up is learning simply to stay put, to not be so "elsewhere" that we are not at home when God comes knocking.[9] That seems painfully simple.

But not always easy to practice.

For one thing, the past keeps pulling us back from the present. I feel hemmed in by who I've been and the choices I've made, convinced I cannot break out of old cycles. Or I spend time regretting dreams that never materialized. Sometimes it's guilt over what I did or left undone, mistakes or sins or lapses. Or what troubles may be anger over someone's betrayal, perhaps something that happened decades ago. Sometimes I struggle to let go of something good from the past that leaves me nostalgic, unwilling to move on. Through these and countless other ways, what *was* rises up in distracting memories that keep me from noticing what awaits *now*. Looking backward steals energy I could use in the light of living day.

And if what lies behind does not trouble, what lies ahead may. I am used to thinking always about the future. When I was younger, with their promise there were milestones ahead. In many ways I hope there still are. But a fixation on the future can deprive me of my present. It tempts me to daydream or worry. "We experience our days as filled with many things to do, people to meet, and appointments to keep," writes Henri Nouwen. "Our lives often seem like overpacked suitcases bursting at the seams. In fact, we are almost always aware of being behind schedule."[10] The unrealized plans and unfinished tasks clutter not only our datebooks but also our souls. It is one thing to live with vision, with a forward outlook;

doing so can demonstrate healthy hope. The problem comes when we stay occupied, forfeiting contentment in the here and now, too tense to receive all that God has for us in this moment. Or, in a different vein, we give too much of ourselves to dreams that do more than motivate us—but consume us. Our musings leave us *pre-occupied*, filling our minds with concerns and ambitions long before we get to where we are going.

My daughter Bekah is learning something about this. For a time she played a kind of game. "Daddy," she'd ask, "what if someone came to you and said you had to give up either your daughter or your wife; who would you give up?" Of course, I would say that I wouldn't let *anyone* force me into that kind of choice. That satisfied her, usually, but sometimes she came back with variations on the question. I know what Bekah was doing: figuring out her place in the scheme of things, processing her fears, testing the safety of her world. It's fine for a child. And the asking of them seemed to help Bekah. This month the fears do not trouble her so much. She acts content to live without too much concern for the uncertainties of her life, any life. But as adults we, too, stew on our own "what ifs?" "Will I lose my job tomorrow? Next year?" "What if I have no food tomorrow?" "What if my spouse leaves me?" "What if my medical insurance gets canceled?" All these questions, understandable as they are, make us unfree, in a way. They keep us always focused on what could happen. They cloud our seeing of what does happen—in the moment. Focusing too much on such questions loads the worries of a larger future onto our mental mainframe. And it slows down our mental processing, robs our joy. This is not to suggest we ignore our fears, but rather that we do not greet them unquestioningly. We ask if they are distracting us with the possibilities of later and, thereby, stealing from us the pleasures of now. We let them drive us to prayer, not worry.

In the here and now, any of us can be more fully present. Living in the present tense helps us release our grasp on what cannot be changed yesterday. We let go of what cannot be orchestrated tomorrow. And we simply receive, in gratitude and in trust. "There are no moments which are not filled with God's infinite holiness," wrote Jean-Pierre de Caussade, "so that there are none we should not honor."[11] De Caussade even wrote of "the *sacrament* of the present moment"—the divine potential in each instant.[12] He meant the very place we are, the very things we do can mediate God's presence. God comes to us where we are, when we are.

In *A Christmas Memory*, Truman Capote's young narrator, Buddy, tells of a disappointing Christmas: "Socks, a Sunday school shirt, some handkerchiefs, a hand-me-down sweater and a year's subscription to a religious magazine for children. . . . It makes me boil." But then he and his friend, an elderly cousin who lives in the same household, go to fly kites. They go to a pasture, and "there," Capote writes, "plunging through the healthy waist-high grass, we unreel our kites, feel them twitching at the string like sky fish as they swim into the wind." The story continues:

> "My, how foolish I am!" my friend cries, suddenly alert, like a woman remembering too late she has biscuits in the oven. "You know what I've always thought?" she asks in a tone of discovery, and not smiling at me but at a point beyond. "I've always thought a body would have to be sick and dying before they saw the Lord. . . . But . . . I'll wager

at the very end a body realizes the Lord has already shown Himself. That things as they are"—her hand circles in a gesture that gathers clouds and kites and grass . . . "—just what they've always been, was seeing Him. As for me, I could leave the world with today in my eyes."[13]

That angle of vision makes all the difference.

We need more than a simple decision to focus on the present, however, as though it takes only a simple mental trick. The pull of the past and our anxiety about the future are not effortlessly shaken off. It takes more than willpower; we need healing for the past and trust for the future. And those come from outside ourselves: from God. To live in the present we must know that God forgives and heals yesterday's sins and hurts, that God orders and watches over tomorrow's uncertainties. Only then does the soul find freedom from regret and fear. No wonder Jesus said to people so often, "Your sins are forgiven." No wonder he told his followers, "Seek first [God's] his kingdom and his righteousness, and all these things will be given to you as well. Therefore do not worry about tomorrow" (Matthew 6:33–34).

I sometimes struggle through life, not as aware of God as I can be, painfully aware, rather, of me. I sometimes relive old hurts and failings. Or I get anxious for what's around the corner. How much time I spend worrying, as I prepare to teach a class, how it will be received! And once done, I sometimes worry if I captivated my audience or touched a life. So much distracts me from full concentration. So much keeps me from enjoying the daily, momentary pleasures of putting words to paper, teaching a workshop of eager learners, letting my seven-year-old daughter read to me at day's end.

When I live in the present, however, the past and the future take their proper places. The past becomes a source of glad memory, not stifling compulsion. Through memory I can relive the joys, relearn the old lessons, take heart from the times God proved faithful. And the future beckons as something not to control or fear, but a path to be walked with trust and courage. A way paved by One we know to be loving and kind.

Living in the here and now is like driving a car at night, to borrow an analogy from novelist E. L. Doctorow. You drive only as far as the headlights allow. But if you keep driving to the edge of what you see you will eventually make the whole trip. So I try to follow the light I have. And it's enough.

WATCH WITH EXPECTANCY

We all have stretches where life seems plain, ordinary. As we grow older we understand that life is not always a backyard adventure. We take on responsibilities. We get pulled along by an undertow of routine and duty. Perhaps a job asks more of us than we want to give. And not all of our ambitions find fulfillment. Learning to live with limits is part of the work of maturing, seeing and accepting life in its modesty as still something good and worthwhile.

But while we lay aside some of our grandiose ambitions for ourselves, we need not stop believing that God still has things to show us, new places to lead our souls. Life is "just a bunch of stuff that happens," says one character on TV. But not when we have eyes to see. Not when we cultivate a childlike watchfulness. Not when we believe that God inhabits each day because there is no place God is not, so there is no moment when God is not. That makes me want to keep my eyes open. While I focus my energies on the present moment, the little task, the ordinary act of faithfulness, I stay expectant.

"You see, but you do not observe," Sherlock Holmes pointed out to Watson. The quick look as we run from one task to another is all we get. But to open our spiritual eyes is to go beyond the surface to catch the unfolding promise of ordinary, flat circumstances.

Diane Eble, author of *Abundant Gifts*, calls this a "habit of seeing." "Once you start looking for daily gifts," Diane said to me once, "you realize they are there." We "take notice of wonder," in Jewish theologian Abraham Heschel's memorable phrase. After all, we tend to see what we train our eyes to see; an architect walks into a room and sees the way the walls are framed, the subtle structural flaws; an interior designer sees color schemes and fabrics and window coverings. In the same way, a spiritually minded person learns to see constant evidences of God. Traces of divine goodness. Markers of a Presence that infuse everything and color what happens next.

My son Micah is taking an art class. The burden of the lessons, at least at this stage, is not so much techniques—feathering with a brush or capturing the interplay of light and shadow—but learning, sometimes *re*learning, how to *see*. The other day the teacher had Micah paint a chrysanthemum—without his looking at his paper. He was to rivet his eyes on the flower, on its multilayered ridges of petals, to concentrate only on the image he was trying to transpose. Well, his efforts, usually wonderful, would win no awards with this jagged attempt. The lines did not all meet; in places the drawing looked like a scribble. But the idea wasn't to reproduce a perfect image on paper. It was to nudge Micah to look more closely, more truly. He was learning to draw from perception, not habit. His teacher would not allow him to reduce his work to lines and shading before he sees. So, writes one artist, "The painter draws with his eyes, not with his hands. Whatever he sees, if he sees it *clear,* he can put down. The putting of it down requires, perhaps, much care and labor, but no more muscular agility than it takes for him to write his name. Seeing *clear* is the important thing."[14] That's what Micah is learning. That's what I am learning.

Sometimes I think I already know, already have in view what God is doing. But often I need to pause, slow down, *watch*. I need to be freed from my habits of conventional looking. I need to see afresh. And as that ability to see God's hand at work in the events around me sharpens, I will become more alert, more awake.

As a child I went some time without knowing how nearsighted I was. I had nothing else to compare my focus with. I must have finally flunked a vision test at school or found myself unable to read the teacher's blackboard handwriting. From the time I went to the optometrist's office to get fitted for glasses until the time they came, I wondered what it would be like to see like people said I should.

The balmy California morning my parents took me to pick the glasses up, I made a discovery. My new lenses not only made things sharper, they caused things to appear I had never seen before. From what had been only a roadside blur emerged words on a sign. What before had been only a distant smudge emerged as rock formations in the craggy hills surrounding our valley.

Looking back, I realize how my newfound vision was a grace. Squinting my eyes or staring harder didn't make the difference. Something enabled me to see. Something outside of myself reoriented my sight. Much of watching likewise has simply to do with a new way of looking. I ask God for vision to see. "The real voyage of discovery consists not in seeking new landscapes but in having new eyes," said novelist Marcel Proust. Eyes that are new because God blesses the seeing.

So I try to pray and look. Sometimes in my mind I go on what pastor and TV show host David Mains calls a "God hunt"; at the end of each day he tries to see where God has been active. Where at least glimmers of His working have shown through the routine. I start at least some days breathing, "God, I want to see you at work."

Doing so asks for a certain deliberateness, of course. It means a conscious decision to look for God, just as in childhood I lifted up rocks when I was hunting centipedes and beetles and pill bugs in my backyard, hoping to see something new. Something similar motivates a friend of mine; he begins his day saying, "Lord, I want your understanding. I want to see through your eyes." That is a good prayer. In the midst of discouragement or boredom, we say to ourselves, *God is somewhere in the midst of this, waiting to be detected.* And we learn (or try) to trust enough to believe there will be something to see.

"For years," writes Kathleen Norris, "early morning was a time I dreaded. In the process of waking up, my mind would run with panic. All the worries of the previous day would still be with me, spinning around with old regrets as well as fears for the future. I don't know how or when the change came, but now when I emerge from night, it is with more hope than fear. I try to get outside as early as possible so that I can look for signs of first light, the faint, muddy red of dawn."[15]

· · ·

Years ago I saw a performance of Thornton Wilder's play *Our Town*. In one scene the young woman who died in childbirth has joined the dead, who ring the stage, observing from their vantage point with growing disinterest the life they left behind. But Emily, new to the dead, still feels the pull and tug of life. When told she can revisit at will the life she just left, she is eager.

The other dead who preceded her, especially her mother-in-law, try to talk her out of it. But she persists. She goes back. And then discovers a sorrow.

"I can't look at everything hard enough," she cries. She breaks down in sobs. "I didn't realize. So all that was going on and we never noticed." Emily says good-bye one last time to her home, to food and coffee and new-ironed dresses.

Then Emily looks to a cast member, the "stage manager" who narrates the story. She blurts, "Do any human beings ever realize life while they live it—every, every minute?"

"No," comes the reply. "The saints and poets, maybe—they do some."[16]

I love that scene. But the answer to Emily's question is a bit more hopeful. It's not just the saints and poets who "realize life" while they live it. It is any who want to see God. A God who does not go into hiding. A God for whom the game of hide and seek has to do with us who hide, with him who seeks, who speaks, who shows up.

In a way, my first visit back home after I married Jill, the visit I opened this chapter with, is with me still.

I have a snapshot on my desk that Jill took the last day of our

visit. I stand with my parents in front of the house, the morning
Santa Monica sun almost glinting off my dad's forehead. Dad holds
Micah, just two years old at the time, while Abram stands by his
granddad. I'm next to my mom and dad, smiling. I've kept the
photo framed and on a desk or dresser all these years. It reminds me
of more difficult times and of answers to prayer. I don't want to
forget any of it. But mostly the picture makes me want to listen and
watch for God's goodness, here and now.

Chapter 4

EYES AND EARS

It is such a very simple thing to walk through life with my hands open, my eyes open, listening, alive in all my five senses to God breaking in again and again on my daily life.
ESTHER DE WAAL[1]

And here in dust and dirt, O here
The lilies of his love appear.
GEORGE HERBERT

$\mathcal{N}ot$ long ago someone called to recruit me to collaborate on a book. I must have sounded noncommittal on the phone. Even wary. But because a significant portion of my income comes from writing, the more I thought about the project, the more I wondered, *Should I call back with more interest?* I didn't want to greet a promising opportunity with indifference.

Restless, I went out into the December late-afternoon air to think. I took the road in front of my house that winds down a gentle hill. Along the rise of hills to the west I saw scattered houses and a ridge of distant, silhouetted trees. My eyes traveled over miles of Tennessee countryside in the valley below. Most dazzling of all, a vast sunset stretched across and above the horizon. The clouds had become marbleized with shades of salmon, azure, and rose pink, backlit with an intensity to rival any cathedral stained glass. I thought of my friend Mary Lee, who had just the day before told me of a Bible verse that called clouds "wonders of him who is perfect in knowledge."

What I remember most, however, was a sudden, glorious assurance about my role in the project I worried about. The God who could fling colors across the panoply of sky before me could easily oversee the nagging details of my life—finances and all. Whatever happened, whether I collaborated or not, I need not worry. I walked back home with senses on high alert and a heart at peace.

When I notice, the concrete realities and wonders of everyday life remind me of things I need to know. Sometimes, of course, I go about my activities with senses dulled, like the man who ran into the Louvre Museum in Paris, breathless, blurting out, "Quick, where's the *Mona Lisa*? I'm double-parked outside." But when I don't rush, my eyes and ears and fingertips help orient my soul. Eating, listening to music, taking a walk help wake me up. An afternoon spent at an art museum or an evening concert of electrifying music can do it. The textures of a painting, the strains of a fiddle, the aroma of baking bread, the caress of spring breezes, the rhythm of verse: I let them declare unseen glories and impress larger truths. I "read" a deeper meaning into the loveliness of a symphony, a blossoming dogwood, a dramatic play. "One's mind," writes scholar C. S. Lewis, "runs back up the sunbeam to the sun."[2] The moon and stars, the glories of harmony, the interplay of a painter's palette of colors remind one of God's creative glories. They are a kind of sign language in which God expresses Himself.

More often than not, we get our snatches of art and beauty when going about our daily lives. When I'm at my desk, music— folk, baroque, Celtic, rock—often plays in the background, an echo of a composer and conductor of infinite melody. My desk furniture is mostly wood, with real grain exposed to sight and touch. There are the grandeurs of the created world just outside my window in the small town south of Nashville I've called home for four years. And there is the steady turning of seasons. I will never forget the spring I fell for Jill; our walks along the suburban streets of Princeton, New Jersey, not far from our grad school campus, were filled with sunshine, the sweet flowery fragrance of rhododendrons, and a joyous awakening to love.

Wherever I live, whatever the time of year, what I see, taste, and touch can point my soul, if I let it, to a new awareness of God's creative goodness. We behold God through His beauty, someone once said. Through it we see traces of the God who created the world and pronounced it good.

I find this liberating. Sometimes I've been tempted to view my bodily senses as distractions. My first inclination is to distrust them. I suppose, as Evelyn Underhill writes, that I must "slink . . . away from the actual to enjoy the eternal."[3] What I touch and see and hear threatens to compete with the work of "interior" formation. Growth becomes a largely mental process, disconnected from concrete realities. I avoid the heresy of the second-century sect known as the Gnostics, teaching that matter is evil, God remote, and salvation available only to those who transcended their earthly bodies with esoteric knowledge. But I still ignore my experience of daily things as an avenue for the soul's growth.

Admittedly, the body's whims and wants can become ends in themselves. Sometimes I enjoy the creature comforts of middle-class life in ways that have more to do with indulging myself than pleasing God. And I know that enjoying the world around me can become a secular, not sacred, experience. "One could, if one practiced," C. S. Lewis wrote, "hear simply a roar and not the roaring-of-the-wind. In the same way, only far too easily, one can concentrate on the pleasure of an event in one's own nervous system . . . and ignore the smell of Deity that hangs about it."[4]

By themselves, then, my senses will not lead me into all truth. I cannot follow their call slavishly. Some dark mornings I know I will give up the soft comfort of my bed to have time to pray. It's not always easy; something beyond immediate sensation moves me. Or, amid a hectic day, when only quiet will give me space to breathe and think about God, I may need to switch off the enticing distraction of the stereo. I choose the harder thing that will fulfill more. Occasionally, I even give up a meal or two to allow me to tame the consuming appeal of food, its preparation, its cleanup. The goodness of hot soup or sweet chocolate tempts me, but I know that fasting—withdrawing occasionally from what is comfortable and comforting—can sharpen my alertness. So for Lent this year, the forty-day period in the Christian calendar leading up to Easter, I have followed a centuries-old custom of giving up a regular pleasure. This year it's been radio and newspapers. I get an urge, every now and then, to flip on the morning news as I do breakfast chores. But my missing it these weeks will allow me to appreciate it more when my media fast is done. The feast of Easter seems all the more glorious because it follows the fast of Lent. *Asceticism,* the strand of spirituality that emphasizes discipline and self-denial, has a place—especially when *sensualism* falsely promises fulfillment. Especially when doing only what gratifies our senses can lead to dark addictions, cutting us off from others, from ourselves, from God.

Modern life presents yet another challenge to employing our senses in spiritual growth. Our senses easily become overwhelmed. Stimuli bombard us faster than we can assimilate them—through fax, phone, e-mail, cable channels, mailboxes. An overloaded system has trouble taking in more—even what could be the restful and hopeful signs of God's drawing near.

But that our body's signals to the soul get distorted or overburdened only points to the power and potential there in the first place. "Our sensuality," writes pastor and teacher Eugene Peterson, "is not a barrier to spirituality but our only access to it."[5] In God's economy, this-worldly things convey rumors of the otherworldly. The visible advertises the invisible. The God above earthly comprehension resorts to hard and gritty realities to reveal Himself. God even became fully human in one particular person, Christians believe. "That which was from the beginning," wrote an early Christian witness, "which we have heard, which we have seen with our eyes, which we have looked at and our hands have touched—this we proclaim" (1 John 1:1).

So I "taste and see," as the psalmist enjoined, "that the Lord is good." I try to use my senses as resources when the day carries reminders I might only half-notice. I tell myself how the world of granite and grass and human life reveals, not hides, God's glory. Eyes and ears and skin enjoy the world God made.

Several dicta help that happen:

LET YOUR SENSES FEED YOUR PRAYING

Lately my prayer times have become more connected to sight and touch, even taste. This morning, for example, I arose early to sit in silence in my living room before the day began. I first brewed a cup of ginseng and cinnamon tea and lit a small candle that I placed on the table by my chair. To help me focus my praying, I took a knotted cotton string (according to an Eastern Orthodox custom) and gently pulled each of the fifty knots through my fingers, repeating with each knot a simple prayer. This morning it was "Thank you, God." Another morning I might use the "Jesus Prayer": "Lord Jesus Christ, have mercy on me." With the distinct feel of each knot between forefinger and thumb helping to focus my heart and soul, I usually can move on to more spontaneous prayers. I read verses from the Bible with a clearer heart. I enjoy the God I cannot see with my eyes or feel with my hands by being prompted by what I can see and feel.

I like the concreteness of striking the match, touching it to the wick. "The very act of lighting the candle," writes Brother David Steindl-Rast, "is prayer."[6] The sight of the flame helps me when my mind wanders. Even when I'm dim, it burns and gives off its own energy, its own light, signifying and setting apart this space and place as prayer when I get off track. Tom Schwanda, who first mentioned the idea to me, takes it even further: His wife made a stained-glass candleholder to highlight the radiance, to catch the soft light in its colored panes. "As I conclude my prayers for others, especially my family," he tells me, "I pray something like this: 'O Lord, shine your light on our path and guide us today.' When I am finished I extinguish the flame." Tom likes to watch the smoke drift upward. Even this becomes a reminder of prayer, like the incense of the Israelites and other religious traditions rising to the heavens.

Or here is Rick Hamlin, on the staff of a New York magazine, taking the subway to work in bustling Manhattan, using the sights not as diversions but attractions:

> Morning after morning I come to this place in a world
> of distractions, and I pray. I don't clock myself, but I
> use the subway stops as markers, guiding me in my
> ritual. I read from the 181st Street station to the 125th
> Street station, usually from the Bible, occasionally from
> what my wife calls a "God book"—a work by some
> metaphysical sage, recent or not so recent. Then at
> 125th Street I close my eyes. It's the express train, no
> more stops from there to 59th Street. At least five
> minutes . . . of uninterrupted time. This is my time
> for God."[7]

Our need to use more than our brain cells when we pray accounts for much of the world's great art and music. Cathedral architecture, stained-glass windows, chapel ceilings adorned with art, plainsong chants and moving requiems, even the physicality of the bread and wine I take at Communion every Sunday, all help us realize, that is, make *real,* what we believe and long for. Common things help us connect. They become transfigured. I've never been there, but my friend Steve once told me of seeing the statue of Saint Peter at the basilica in Rome. The big toe of the foot bears an unusual mark. Through the centuries countless people have touched or kissed it—wearing it down. I suppose they wanted to feel their way to divine reality. I have never been drawn to venerating statues, certainly not toes, but I know little gestures can make times of prayer a concrete reality, a simple, life-giving ritual. We try to make contact with Mystery by turning to the tangible.

And I know people who sing their prayers, drawing on great hymn traditions, even making up their own as they go. Or they play music with a contemplative, monastic flavor in the background. I know people who, involving their limbs and hands, don't limit themselves to one devotional posture: when they pray or worship they dance or stand, arms outstretched, or lie prostrate. They may even curl into a fetal position. They let the body's attitude convey a deeper reality. Some determine that every time they handle a paper clip at work, they will let that simple, consecrated act remind them to think of God. A friend lets landmarks in his commute jog his memories: "If I pass a church, school, hospital, or courthouse, I pray for the pastors, teachers, students, doctors, nurses, technicians, judges." And at any time, observing a tree or the splashing water of a fountain might point your soul to the God who helps keep you aware. Simple physical acts help your soul stay alert.

It's this way at the church I attend. Stained-glass windows capture telling stories from the Bible and church history in vivid color. It seems quaint, but before entering a pew some members nod their head slightly forward as they bend their knees, acknowledging the holiness of God present. We use "kneelers," most of us, padded platforms at the right height for kneeling so at least some of our time in worship has us bent, bowed, our bodies a kind of prayer in themselves. Such simple movements make the life of my soul seem less divorced from my senses, from my everyday tasks.

LET FOOD NOURISH MORE THAN YOUR BODY

Today the preacher at church recited an ancient biblical story of how God fed the people of Israel with a mysterious substance called manna while they wandered in the desert. Whatever manna was (people debate this), one thing stands out: God would provide what Israel needed, even if it took raining a resinous, mysterious substance on the camps and shrubs. A substance the people gathered and used for food. The story is about more than God's wanting to keep them from physically starving, the preacher said. The story's undercurrents suggest how God fed the people's souls. God gave a reminder of His caring practicality.

After the church service, I found myself sitting at McDonald's, the emblematic fast-food restaurant. My daughter wanted to stop in on the way home from church. She loves the attached playground and likes the fries, which she ordered with a hamburger. I ordered a fried-fish sandwich. Served in cardboard boxes with plastic "silverware," the food could by no stretch be considered an elegant meal. And the surroundings, a glassed-in area with gaudy jungle-gym equipment and shouting, exuberant children, hardly compared with the reverent, restful quiet of church. But I realized that it was good to eat, even fast food. The chipped fish and o verprocessed bun would help supply the energy I needed for the afternoon.

So I ate with my seven-year-old before she ran off to play. Then while she traipsed through the climbing tubes and shimmied down the plastic slides, I began making connections. Today, with manna nowhere in sight, can a meal help me do more than assuage my appetite and satisfy my taste buds? Yes, I realized, God has, once again, kept the specter of hunger at bay, this time through flaky fish and pungent tartar sauce. But even more significant, I realized, eating had became an occasion to think about God and commune with my daughter. I realized that even this meal was a blessing. Even when the bread I broke had more in common with an assembly line than a church sanctuary or baker's hearth.

And then I thought about the "meal" I had joined in at church just before, the one that commemorated Jesus' death and turned my eyes to His return. As I lined up at the front rail at my church, kneeling on the cross-stitched cushions, elbows on the oak rail, the priest placed in my palm a wafer to eat. "The body of Christ, the bread of heaven," I heard him say as he put the thin facsimile of bread in my upturned, cupped palms. An assistant came along with a chalice of wine to sip. "The blood of Christ, the cup of salvation," she said. Many Christians call this kind of ritual consumption on Sunday a "sacrament"—a means of grace, a way to experience Christ's presence in a tangible, concrete way. It is our manna. The Eucharist becomes the soul's bread and drink.

Away from that Sunday, I try to see eating as more and more an occasion to refresh the soul as well as replenish my body. Whether I eat a Communion wafer or crab cake, a fish sandwich on the run or a can of beans cooked over a campfire, food itself mediates God's life-giving care.

I once met the writer and English professor Thomas Howard. He is a dignified man, literate in style and literary in diction. He writes of one particularly hectic day when his wife dryly remarked, "Lunch won't be a ceremonial meal today." Their schedules would allow only a quick sandwich eaten in the kitchen. The conversation sets off a series of ruminations akin to mine:

> Except in the most harried situations, there is more
> occurring than the mere swallowing of food. We mark

this thrice-daily event with certain formalities, no matter how small. We put place mats down or a cloth. We put the fork on the left, even though the chances are that we will pick it up with our right hand. If we have a drink we may raise our glasses briefly. . . . We wait until the others have been served before we tuck in. . . . The chances are that even when we are alone, we do not stand at the stove and fork our food out of the saucepan directly into our mouth."[8]

No, he realizes, even the most unceremonious meals take on a kind of ritual. Why? Because they matter more than we think. They involve more than shoveling in carbohydrates and proteins. No wonder many cultures find identity in recipes and aromas of the kitchen or hearth. So George Greenstein in *Secrets of a Jewish Baker* tells of baking rye bread. He stands in a silent bakery with two hundred loaves he has just taken from the ovens. "When the cold night air hits the hot crusts, they begin to crack—a two-hundred participant symphony of precious sounds. He knows that he has made perfect bread."[9] Or Peter Reinhart, author of *Brother Juniper's Bread Book,* "knows his bread is just right by the crunching sound of the crust when he bites into it."[10] Teeth and tongue tell us of more than chemicals. We are made for communion, which meals can mediate. They remind us of God's delight in providing for us.

When I realize that I am more prone to make everyday meals occasions to remember God's good gifts, I am more likely to want more than convenience. Writes poet and novelist Wendell Berry, "Our kitchens and other eating places more and more resemble filling stations, as our homes more and more resemble motels. 'Life is not very interesting,' we seem to have decided. 'Let its satisfactions be minimal, perfunctory, and fast.' "[11] We "grab a bite" but forfeit richer nourishment. Fewer families and friends actually sit together to eat, it seems. And what we eat often majors in quickness. Like most people, I buy prepackaged food, but not without a hidden cost. The cottony-white, plastic-bagged bread I grab off a grocery shelf bears little resemblance to the yeasty smell, the warm feel, the crunchy shell of just-baked bread.

So this afternoon, making tea before sitting at my desk to write, I boiled my water in a teakettle. I relished hearing the steam escape with a whistle, smelling the aroma of the green tea leaves, getting sticky fingers from the spun honey, stirring in the milk. *If we allowed ourselves more connection to such physical processes,* I thought, *we would have more time to think, to ponder, to enjoy.*

It takes a decision to eat and drink and enjoy one another in grateful reverence. But simple changes in meals—opening our eyes as well as our mouths, listening to our hungry souls as well as our growling stomachs, giving meals time to truly fill us and those we sup with—make the difference. When our family of five gathers for an evening meal, one of us (we take turns) says "grace," a simple prayer of thanks for the table of food we enjoy together. It is not elaborate, but it connects us with one another, with our food, with its Source. After the "Amen," we sometimes find ourselves enjoying the bread and meat of good company, a manna for the soul. Yes, the "I don't like this soup!" from a child sometimes brings an irreverent end to this holy communion. Sometimes I'm distracted or Jill, my wife, is about to rush off to an evening meeting. But even then, even amid our imperfect relating, I try to take note of the larger back-drop, the deeper significance, against which our eating—and even hurrying—can take place.

LET THE WORLD AROUND YOU STUN YOU
WITH REMINDERS OF ITS MAKER

On a cool September day years ago, when I lived in Virginia, I went for a just-barely-dawn run along the wooded road near my house. I happened upon a butterfly perched on the road, wings upfolded, very still. The approach of fall's brisk air left the butterfly sluggish. I marveled at the black wings bordered by a misty blue band; it was a kind I had never seen before. I decided to pick it up. Carefully cupping him as I ran, I brought it home to Abram, just three years old and learning to love the natural world. Abram's exuberant jabbering, I suppose, disturbed the creature from his doldrums. He flew away, leaving shimmery flecks of butterfly dust in my palms. But I suspect it was more than Abram's animated reaction that sent him on his way. It was the dawn's widening warmth, plus the heat from my shielding hands. The butterfly, by the way, was not the only one shaken from dormancy that morning. I can still almost feel the glistening, powdery dust on my palms.

From the beginning of time, the awesome glories of creation, big and small, have caught humankind's reverent attention. The heavens declare the glory of God. Humankind sees and hears and is moved. Paul the apostle wrote, "For since the creation of the world God's invisible qualities—his eternal power and divine nature— have been clearly seen, being understood from what has been made" (Romans 1:20). A tuft of moss on a woodland log; the majesty of rocky peaks; the teeming life of Oregon tidepools; the glory of a cottontail deer, startled by human approach, bounding away; a baby born, miracle of miracles, from the union of two people, all tell us about the infinitely creative imagination of the God who made them. We see a hand behind the handiwork. An Artist revealed in the art. A saying attributed to Saint Francis makes the point: "Sister, speak to me of God, I said to the almond tree, and it blossomed."

Many little things can move us deeper into prayer. As can the awesome vistas. Or the simple glimpses. Louise was sledding one winter night with her boys. In the middle of all the running and laughing, she told me, she took a moment to lie down in the snow and look up at the night sky full of stars. Moments like that, she said, "leave me amazed and in awe of God." No wonder the sixteenth-century French theologian John Calvin wrote, "Wherever you cast your eyes, there is no spot in the universe wherein you cannot discern at least some sparks of [God's] glory."[12]

When I lose track of God, then, sometimes a glance out the car window or a look at a loved one bathed in sunlight can reorient me. Even glimpses stolen from a hectic day put me back in touch. Reconnect me. A skeptic once asked a rabbi, thinking of the story where God appeared to Moses through a bush that caught afire, "Why did God speak to Moses through a burning bush—a mere thornbush?" Answered the rabbi, "To teach you that there is no place on earth where God's glory is not, not even in a humble thornbush." Sometimes a thornbush seems like a wonder in itself, when my eyes truly see. Every day we can almost touch God through the world He has made. "When I consider your heavens," the psalmist wrote, "the work of your fingers, the moon and the stars, which you have set in place, what is man . . . ? O Lord, our Lord, how majestic is your name in all the earth!"

.   .   .

A move to a faraway place left a friend of mine depressed. She thought a few days' vacation on Florida beaches would help cure her griefs and stresses. She didn't realize at first how true that was:

"All that week in Florida I was looking for sand dollars and had only found one. A friend who had found three thought I might have better luck earlier in the day. So on my last morning in Florida I headed out early. I hadn't been on the beach long when I had a *strong* feeling that God wanted me to ask Him for help in finding sand dollars. *How silly,* I thought. *Of course God wouldn't be saying that to me.* But the feeling was so strong that I finally said 'God, I don't even know how to ask. But since you seem to want to help, would you please help me find some?'

"Immediately I noticed off to my right a broken conch shell. I hadn't seen any shells of that type all week. So I bent down to pick it up and there, four inches away, was my first sand dollar. After finding thirteen more, I felt the Lord saying, 'Darla, these sand dollars are like your new home in Philadelphia. You feel like you've only found one sand dollar of beauty there. But I have much more than that for you.'

"Once I got home that evening something else happened. My son Daniel brought down a sand dollar and put it next to mine. When I told the family the story, my husband asked Daniel if he thought it interesting that God had used sand dollars to speak to me. It turns out that months earlier when Daniel was frustrated, angry, and hurting about our coming here he etched 'I hate Philadelphia' into his sand dollar.

"Now I have a sand dollar sitting right here beside the computer. When I was jogging the other day I thought about it and decided I should buy a notebook and write 'sand dollars' on it. I could list every gift of joy and beauty that God shows me here. I still miss my Nashville friends. I know the fruition of God's plans will take time, but a simple find at the seashore helped me rediscover God's incredible comfort."

LET BEAUTY POINT YOU TO GLORIES BEYOND

I am no art connoisseur, musical expert, literary genius. But I know the glories of Handel's *Messiah*, the play of light in a Rembrandt, a powerful movie; even the driving rhythm of a rock band stirs something in me. I let what I experience speak deeply. I try not to get lost in analyzing, but surrender to what the song or quilt or painting or statue can tell me. I try to receive.

Not just raw creation, but all beauty—that which, in varied forms, attracts our senses—has the potential to catch our soul's attention as well. The beautiful can draw our notice away from ourselves, alerting us to God, who, in the words of the Bible, lives in the beauty of holiness. The beautiful wakes us up to a dimension beyond the merely mundane, under the surface. Beauty, in this sense, is not skin deep, but evidence of a God who saturates life with orderliness and admirable form. Art witnesses to the Something More present in any moment, any scene, any life. The violinist's bow or sculptor's chisel coax eternal realities out of hiding.

"In the presence of the beautiful," writes Eugene Peterson, "we intuitively respond in delight, wanting to be involved, getting near, entering in—tapping our feet, humming along, touching, kissing, meditating, contemplating, imitating, believing, praying. Painted prayers; sung prayers; danced prayers. It's the very nature of our senses to pull us into whatever is there—scent, rhythm, texture, vision. . . . [and most] exquisitely beauty that finds its fulfillment in the human face."[13] At those times when I need to be taken out of myself, beauty helps.

I know how beauty affected my former California neighbor. I was visiting in his living room and I commented on a print of a renowned painting on his wall, one of Vincent van Gogh's vases of vivid sunflowers. He then told me a story. Some years earlier, Ron thought his eyesight seemed fuzzied, dimming. A diagnosis of macular degeneration swiftly confirmed his fears of approaching blindness. As a way of coping, he made arrangements to spend a week visiting the Van Gogh museum in Amsterdam. For a week he did nothing but make his way through the museum, soaking up the art, learning about Van Gogh, talking with the curator. He wanted his last glimpses filled with the images of a master, with reflections of creative grandeur. When I saw him, he could barely see the vibrant colors on the print on his wall. But his memory was rich with an artist's evocative skill. I never forgot his story.

Years later, when a Dutch television program flew me to Amsterdam for an interview, I knew I would visit the Van Gogh museum. I wanted to retrace the footsteps of my art-loving friend. While I did not have the dazzling experiences he did (I had only an hour or so before I caught my ride), I could see what drew Ron to the museum. I felt touched by the artist's power to inspire and transform. The great pathos and ecstasy Van Gogh poured onto his canvases made me thoughtful, grateful.

But I cannot visit museums or concert arenas every day. When, as in so many things, the daily realities never match the possibilities, what then?

I remind myself that much of my appreciation of beauty happens wherever I find myself. A simple melody can touch me, if I let it. I don't need a concert hall. A book, cleanly and beautifully designed, can do it. The radiance of an elderly person, wrinkles and all, points to the quieter glories of the universe.

Our inability to notice the aesthetically pleasant has little to do with dimming eyesight or hearing impairment. No, beauty is beheld by those who have learned how to perceive. We *look* for beauty, not just wait for it to conk us on the head. We learn to be patient. In a letter, the poet Rainer Maria Rilke talks about his first exposure to the art of the French impressionist painter Cézanne: "I remember the puzzlement and insecurity of one's first confrontation with his work, along with his name, which is just as new. And then for a long time nothing, and suddenly one has the right eyes."[14] When that happens we see what we would have otherwise missed.

And we must sometimes confess that our perceptions need healing. Because we live in a fallen world, distorted by sin, much of the time we operate with skewed ways of viewing. No wonder the Gospels make much of stories of Jesus healing the deaf and blind. While I believe these are more than mere allegories, but poignant, concrete, very real miracle stories, they also seem to suggest an onionskin layer below the physical. They suggest that our inner seeing and hearing need restoration. Our discernment of the world as it is, in its beauty (and ugliness), has become distorted. If we have not acquired a taste for the holy, evil seems attractive indeed. Good appears bland. So we need to do more than simply try harder to be aware. No, we need a fundamental transformation. "Our senses have been dulled by sin," writes Eugene Peterson. The world, for all its sensuality, "is relentlessly anesthetic, obliterating feeling by ugliness and noise, draining the beauty out of people and things." It turns people into functions, beauty into commodities. Unredeemed senses grow impatient with the beautiful "except as it can be contained in a museum or flower garden."[15] Without healing, we will rush to possess, spoiling what we see or hear with our acquisitiveness.

But offering our eyes and ears and pores to God, we find our perceptions becoming finer. "If the doors of our perception were cleansed," wrote poet and artist William Blake, "we would see the world as it is, infinite." Then a dimension, there all along, emerges in clear view, right where we are. Jesus said that the pure in heart will see God. He might have also said that they will see the beauty of God. When we ask God to show Himself in the world around us, He will.

Wrote Elizabeth Barrett Browning,

Earth's crammed with heaven,
And every common bush afire with God;
But only he who sees takes off his shoes;
The rest sit around and pluck the blackberries.[16]

When you are looking for someone you are supposed to meet and pick up in a train station or airport terminal, you skim your eyes across countless faces. But if you concentrate, you will notice only one face, only your loved one's voice calling across the terminal. What we condition our eyes and ears and hearts to find affects what we see.

Much the same could be said about beauty, and the Face it reveals, when we have the sense to see and wherewithal to hear. We find ourselves nudged to prayerful awareness. And in prayer our eyes and ears and mouths become conditioned more and more to take in what can, if we let it, move us and remake us.

Chapter 5

The
Soul
AND THE
SIMPLE LIFE

Do not give your heart to that which does not satisfy your heart.
ABBA POEMAN

The great danger facing all of us is . . . that some day we may wake up and find that always we have been busy with the husks and trappings of life—and have really missed life itself.
PHILLIPS BROOKS

One recent morning I wakened earlier than normal, unable to go back to sleep. This meant that instead of rushing around to rouse my fourteen-year-old from bed, pack Bekah's school bag, and get myself ready for work, I moved at a more leisurely pace. Spreading butter on Bekah's bread felt more relaxed. I noticed how much more *aware* I was: the soft, springy feel of the bread, the pleasure of making a meal for a child, the gentle dawn light outside in the yard. Later, during my lunch hour that day, walking the street near the office where I worked, I noticed the budding maples, the cool air, the brilliant sunshine.

What if I got up early more often? I wondered. But that didn't explain the difference in my morning, not really. The question went deeper: What if my life was not so crammed with hurried tasks? And deeper still: Why does life seem full but only occasionally fulfilling? Why do so many homes have refrigerator calendars so chocked full of activities that the mind boggles at getting it all done?

"The simple life" has held our fascination for decades. It seems to promise the answer for questions like mine. The media feeds us stories about high-powered entrepreneurs and advertising executives who call it quits. In quest of sanity, they "downscale" and move to quieter towns or farms to live closer to nature. Some write books about their discoveries, like college professor Bernd Heinrich. Heinrich spent an entire year, hermitlike, in a New England cabin with no running water or electricity, perched near a brook and the Presidential Mountains. I bought his book, *A Year in the Maine Woods*, charmed by the account of a life freed from filling out forms, reading memos, and sitting in meetings.[1] Henry David Thoreau's *Walden,* which I read like countless other high school juniors in literature class, likewise tantalizes us with the possibilities of scaling back and making a roomier life. We sense our lives brim with material abundance but not abundant life. We want more richness, less clutter. At least some days we would nod in agreement to hear commentator Michael Novak say, "the aftertaste of affluence is boredom." Life's many gadgets and marvels by themselves leave us wanting. "I woke up one morning," reflected one business executive, "and I realized I was never going to make a million dollars, my marriage was never going to meet my wildest expectations, my children were grown and didn't need me anymore—and this was going to be all there was." We feel something missing amid the many things.

It's tempting to think a stripping down to material basics would cure us. That cutting back our time commitments would save us. Whatever the truth to that, the answer requires more profound explorations.

THINK OUTLOOK, NOT JUST LIFESTYLE

I walk around my bedroom, which for now doubles as my writing study. In a corner sits an oak desk, a computer, and a pine library table piled with books. It looks as if it was shoehorned into the room, as my writing has been over the years. In many ways the room seems like a microcosm of my world—even my daily life having odds and ends squeezed in wherever they fit.

On the wall facing me, I have hung matted and framed covers of books I've authored. There is a magazine cover with my name featured prominently as the author of one of the stories. They loom large on the wall and encourage me as I write, reminding me of past successes. What I find more fascinating, however, is the little icon of Jesus on the table to my left, propped up against some books. That's where my eye wanders most frequently. Painted in muted reds, greens, and golds in traditional Eastern Orthodox style, Jesus stands with a gently enigmatic expression, hand held up in a gesture of priestly blessing. Mounted on an oak slab, the portrait is not much larger than a postcard. But it suggests immense meanings. I'm told the Greek letters in the large halo stand for "One Who Is." I find that comforting. No wonder I find myself drawn to the face:

One who is, which also suggests *one who was, and who will be.* And then my eye goes back to my covers on the wall, the desk, the accumulating files, symbolizing my career aspirations. Am I in some human sense striving to be One Who Is? I realize anew where I should put my gaze.

I get up to look through my side of the large walk-in closet I share with my wife, on the opposite side of the room. I discover my pants and shirts and jackets use up over sixty hangers, and that's not counting sweaters and sweat pants stored in drawers. I have a studied way to dress for every effect: conservatively professional, fashionably casual, even grungy. Jeans, suits, polo shirts. I dress one way for this crowd, another for that. I'm not obsessed with clothes. But still I wonder: How much energy do I expend making sure I look just right? Am I too distracted by how I "come off"?

Much vies for my attention. In my work, in my daily relationships, in so many areas, I find myself identifying with the late priest and author Henri Nouwen:

> Reflecting on my . . . work, I realize more and more
> that it lacked unity. . . . Now I see that I was all
> mixed up, that I had fragmented my life into many
> sections that did not really form a unity. . . . My
> fears and the resulting fatigue over the last three years
> might well be diagnosed as a lack of single-
> mindedness, as a lack of one-eyedness, as a lack of
> simplicity. I want to love God, but also make a
> career. . . . I want to be a saint, but also enjoy the
> sensations of the sinner. No wonder that living
> becomes a tiring enterprise. . . . I . . . have a very
> divided loyalty.[2]

But I also see other possibilities for my life, possibilities I manage to keep in view some of the time, at least. I knew a nun once who did also. In the days before computers replaced typewriters, she was typing out a snatch of a psalm. She intended to type the verse that asks God, "Create in me a clean heart." But she punched a wrong key and ended up with *clear* heart. "I don't know that that was such an accident after all," she told me. "My heart needs to be cleared of distractions so I can hear what the Lord is saying."

Much of simplifying means praying for a clear heart. An undivided soul. Before I grow overly concerned about how many (or few) changes of clothes I own, about whether I make my own granola and bake my own bread, I clarify where I put my fundamental focus. Simplicity may well mean spending less at the shopping mall. It almost always means giving priority to intangibles like family and friends. But the controlling metaphor is not a calculator as much as a compass. We simplify when we settle where life comes from and where it heads toward. A corporate consultant I know tells his client businesses, "What matters most is not perfection, but direction."

In books on simplifying you often find practical advice—getting off junk-mail lists that leave you barraged with catalogs and offers, cutting back on credit purchases, avoiding overly packaged prepared foods. I appreciate any practical advice I can get. Every time my family and I move (and my wife and I have moved nine times in twenty years of marriage), I am amazed at how much stuff we own. As the saying goes, "Three moves is as good as a fire." Even so, the boxes and piles of belongings seem like dead weight when it is time to pick up and leave some place. How tethered we seem, bound to a home by all we own. We live in a roomy house that we enjoy. But some boxes sit stored in our garage unopened since the last move several years ago. Books, my prized possessions, threaten to inundate our bedroom. I need release from what the Quakers call "cumber." Send in a "clutter counselor," to use the trendy expression.

But I also know that such advice doesn't go far enough. Not for me. Not with my divided loyalties. I could strip my material life to barest essentials and still stir a cauldron of ambitions, secret jealousies, and anxious plays for approval. How often do I care more for my appearance than how I can help someone in need! In a group of people where something goes wrong, I scheme to cover my tracks. I want too badly to look good. Or I get ambitious, relishing the glow of feeling good about my accomplishments, my books in print, my byline. I like to be recognized as talented. Knowing me, a mere program of steps to simplicity is liable to let me think I simplify when in truth I merely substitute new regimens or personal ambitions. It would only give me new ways to put proud notches in my belt.

No, more than a series of steps, I need a simplicity that grows out of a state of heart—a condition of soul. My finding a simpler, calmer life has mostly to do with my honoring what Karl Barth called our "incurable God-sickness." My homesickness for the Holy. "God is the only Reality," said Augustine, "and we are only real in so far as we are in His order and He in us." That's why the icon of Jesus on my table most moves me. When I clarify my direction, when I try to live for God, life gains a new sense of focus. The activities, problems, and anxieties begin to fit into place. An inner order replaces the internal striving. Things come 'round right.

This has not become a constant state of grace for me. Becoming simple is complicated. For one thing, I must contend with the many parts and sides of me. Each person, writes Quaker Thomas

Kelly, "tends to be, not a single self, but a whole committee of selves." He theorizes that in a way we have a civic self, parental self, religious self, financial self. All vie for dominance. If I serve on a community committee, I feel guilty for not being home. If I spend time with my family, I feel as if I should give more time to the world's needy. If I spend money for a pair of running shoes not on sale, a part of me feels extravagant. I feel divided. Our many interests become distractions, not expressions of a single purpose. They reflect, writes Kelly, "an inner lack of integration of our own lives. We are trying to be several places at once, without all our selves being organized by a single, mastering Life within us."[3]

A single, mastering Life provides the soul's true simplicity. That is where peace comes from. When I was a child, I would get so completely absorbed in my play that I forgot everything else. At that moment, I didn't worry if my Erector set contraption or crayoned tree and scrawled clouds won an award. I lived from a playful, unself-conscious center. I became lost in my focus. But I did not *lose* anything; I was fully myself. If I could now, as an adult, live with more of that simple, childlike clarity, if I could trust God to lead, many of my tensions would be exposed as empty, unnecessary worries. Many of my distractions would dissolve.

Another analogy comes to mind. Those who feel the urge to lead a good life, said the medieval spiritual writer Meister Eckhart, should do what the person does who wants to draw a perfect circle. First the person fixes the center point of the compass. "Only then," said Eckhart, "will he be able to draw a perfect circle." Likewise the person "must learn in the first place to fix his heart on God, the center, and thereby on all good works and everything good." We start with the center point, not the periphery. We live at the level of the heart, not the surface.

But how?

Once, a teacher in Jesus' day, mystified by the many rules of religious life he was expected to follow, asked Jesus, "Of all the commandments, which is the most important?" I can picture how harried he felt from the multiplied customs of first-century religious life. I can imagine how divided his life may have felt.

"The most important one," answered Jesus, "is this: 'Hear, O Israel, the Lord our God, the Lord is one. Love the Lord your God with all your heart and with all your soul and with all your mind and with all your strength.' The second is this: 'Love your neighbor as yourself.' There is no commandment greater than these" (Mark 12:28–31).

You could not have asked for a simpler answer.

Or a harder one. What Jesus pointed my restless heart to means I will, when not lulled by society's version of the "good life," live for Another above and beyond me. I will get clear about who the audience is I play to—the audience of One, as someone put it. I will allow myself to be guided as much by a concern for others' welfare as for my own. I find all that intimidating. I suppose everyone does. *All* my heart and soul and mind and strength? This is no polite religion, no God as hobby. Love another as much as I love *me?* This is an outlook that turns upside down any careful approach.

But still I try. What I am trying to describe—trying to live— doesn't ignore the many and constant demands of our lives. It provides a context for them. I try to "consolidate" the many anxieties and find simply myself anxious for God's kingdom. We learn to listen to what Thomas Kelly called the "welling-up whispers" of God's guidance, love, and presence.[4] Living for God first is, in some ways, more complicated than simply signing on to a program. Cut-and-dried rules on how much we can responsibly spend on a car purchase in some ways would be easier. This requires a different kind of effort, and perhaps mistakes and surprises. But it promises truly to help us.

Recently I attended a committee meeting at a publishing company. A colleague, John Mogabgab, the editor of a spiritual-life publication, was describing how he and his staff had recently got away from the office for a planning retreat. They hoped to become more focused for their work, he said. At one point in the retreat, John recounted, someone mentioned the story of Mary and Martha in the Bible.

Immediately my mind went to the scene: Jesus visiting with two sisters. Martha acts beside herself, worrying over her hospitality. She frantically complains to Jesus about her sister Mary, sitting at Jesus' feet, just listening to him talk. "Martha, Martha," Jesus chides her, "you are worried and upset about many things, but only one thing is needed" (Luke 10:41–42). That story, John said, became a focal point for the retreat. The leader of the retreat posed the question to John and his staff: "What is the one needed thing?"

John had no idea what happened in me at the mention of that question. Out of the blue it hit me with surprising force: *What is the one needed thing?* The committee meeting went on, but I was moved almost to tears. I couldn't understand fully why. Except that my life then seemed a bit like a jumble of activities and scattered interests. I needed a more focused outlook. Something about the mere question made that clear.

Driving home that evening from the office, I realized that I filled my life with many "needed things"—home schooling my fifteen-year-old, working part-time, writing a book, maintaining a house, keeping up with my hobbies and reading—but too often neglected the *one* thing. It seemed partly a clarifying of how I spent my work time—my calling to write and teach about prayer. I prayed about making practical changes in my life to ensure that calling the space it needed. But the larger sense wasn't so much that I had to give up the things I was doing. The "one thing," most of all, had to be living for God. That was what I was neglecting, in some way I could barely articulate.

So here I am, months later, still concerned about getting ahead in my career, wanting to be praised as the next great spiritual-life writer. But a stronger part of me wants to live with single focus. I stumble, but as I make steps forward I discover, as Simone Weil did, that "Nothing is so beautiful and wonderful, nothing is so continually fresh and surprising, so full of sweet and personal ecstasy, as the good." When I realize that, the good, God Himself, seems well worth all my soul's delighted attention. God keeps patiently reminding me that I can do no better than to live with Him and toward Him.

CULTIVATE CONTENTMENT

I know of an African-American man who lived through many of the indignities visited upon blacks in this country. He grew up prior to civil rights reforms and lived through the violent, painful struggles of those decades, struggles that are with us still. And while he suffers from painful, debilitating rheumatoid arthritis, while he is old, you can sense a remarkable calmness about him. He will tell you it has to do with his grateful, contented heart. "Gratitude," he says, "prepares the eye and ear of the heart to see and hear God."

Simplicity has much to do with contentment. I am more likely to buy what I don't need and accumulate clutter when I'm agitated. I am more likely to elbow somebody for possessions when I am not "centered down." I will think that happiness is just a purchase away. This course, this book, this vacation, we say to ourselves, will answer the restless desire. And some things we do legitimately need. We can acquire them with perfect freedom. But we also know that, as Marjorie Thompson writes, "there is a vacuum inside us that will suck up an infinite supply of thrills, goods, and successes without satisfying the . . . heart."[5] The size of a person's paycheck, surveys and studies show, has little bearing on happiness. Above the poverty level there is scant correlation between income and contentment. But the act of thanking, however much or little someone owns, an attitude of gratitude, that is another matter.

My Thanksgiving holiday this year was a simple affair. In contrast to many years, my family and I traveled to no relatives' house. We had no friends over. It was just the five of us. We spent the day mostly together, chopping, cooking, baking, preparing. Then we sat down to eat while pies cooled on a rack—turkey, sweet potatoes, homemade cranberry relish, oatmeal buns. It was simple, and we simply enjoyed one another's presence.

As darkness descended, we gathered around a fire my children had built in the fireplace. We talked, watched the flames, sat back, full and content. Then Bekah taught us a song she had learned at school, a song that acknowledged we all have things to be thankful for, and whose refrain led to the line, "Let me tell you what they are."

That line was a cue for one of us to name something he or she was grateful for. Then the song began again, stopping with the next person's turn to call out a blessing. I don't remember everything we said. Often we called out the usual: a house to live in, a guitar to play (from my musical oldest son), one another.

But I was struck by how easy it was to keep it going. We decided to quit singing eventually, but not before we went through many rounds. We never ran out of things to mention. And I suspect I could do that every day.

This morning I decided, whenever I felt an impulse to pray, as much as I could, only to utter words of thanks. Going about my duties, writing a book, arranging the family's complicated needs for rides here and there, planning supper, I found within a quiet, unexplainable, and unexpected contentment. Life seemed simpler indeed, for all the deadline pressures I face, for all the family responsibilities I feel. I don't agree with those who say that thanks and praise represent the most "mature" prayers; we need never hesitate to employ a rich variety of prayers—including passionate prayers for justice and change. But I sometimes forget how thankfulness provides the backdrop for a life lived with God.

This has implications for how we pray every day. For years I have kept a prayer list: a sheet or index card to help remind me to pray for certain people and situations. Not many months ago I turned over my card of requests and wrote at the top of the blank side THANKSGIVING. And then I listed all that I am grateful for: a loving wife, children doing well in school, book projects to keep me busy, a house and neighborhood to live in. That morning I started the part of my prayer time where I pray for specific things with thanks. And whenever I can get such focused times for prayer, I try to remember to start with the side that lists what I already enjoy, the gifts showered on my life and the lives of those I love. Then I turn to the urgent needs. The practice helps me not become whiny. "Gratitude," writes Thomas Merton, "takes nothing for granted, is never unresponsive, is constantly awakening to new wonder and to praise of the goodness of God."[6]

Perhaps you heard the story of King Pyrrhus. Having decided to invade Italy, he sent for Cineas, a philosopher and the king's friend. "What do you think of my plan?" he asked.

"Why do you want to invade it?" Cineas asked.

"To conquer it."

"Then what will you do?" Cineas continued.

"Go into France."

"And then what?"

"Conquer Spain," said the king.

"I gather you want to conquer the whole world," replied the philosopher. "What will you do when you have conquered all?"

"Why, then," said the king, "we will return and enjoy ourselves in quiet in our own land."

"So may you now," said Cineas, "without all this ado."

Each of us has a voice inside of us like Cineas. A voice that reminds us that amid whatever we have now, the plot we till, the relationships we nurture, the skills we have, the house or apartment we inhabit, we can find contentment. We still the voices that would agitate us, drive us, convince us we must always have something more.

We will still tend to conjugate our lives around verbs such as "to make," "to accomplish," "to have," "to enlarge." We like to have things to show for our efforts. We strive for more, for faster, and especially for bigger. And therein lies much of our stress. But what attracts me about simplicity is not the premise that I should list what I can do without but the promise that I can become more aware of what I already have. And then I will care less about hoarding or having to have the latest model. I will feel more freedom to share with another. I will be more willing to give, even when it requires a sacrifice, for I will be giving not grudgingly, but gratefully, not out of perceived lack, but true abundance.

REMEMBER HOW LESS IS MORE
AND LITTLE IS LARGE

I have lost the art of enjoying many simple pleasures. Numbed as I sometimes feel by a world of blaring volume and frenetic video motion, I seem to feel less. Our modern senses get so sated that we no longer notice the small and truly prized. We stop seeing and enjoying delights that are only seemingly ordinary.

Sometimes we can't see what we have because of the sheer quantity of goods. The accumulating piles hide and obscure. "A home is like a reservoir equipped with a check valve," wrote E. B. White. "The valve permits influx but prevents outflow. Acquisition goes on day and night—smoothly, subtly, imperceptibly. I have no sharp taste for acquiring things, but it is not necessary to desire things in order to acquire them." Goods seek us out, he said, even though our guard is up. We get things in the mail. Offers and sales seem too good to pass up. "The steady influx," he says, "is not counterbalanced by any comparable outgo."[7] And so we find ourselves trapped or at least distracted by a disorienting jumble.

Holly Cumming, a middle-aged office-organizing consultant I know, recently spent a weekend at a monastery in rural Kentucky. She was awed by the silence and simplicity of the place, especially by the chapel, its clean, spare lines, and the monks, with their simple attire and soft chanting. To be outside was to be surrounded by the unadorned beauty of nature. "How clear, clean, and simple it all seemed," she told me. "I realized how much the monks did with so little. And I was struck by how relaxed it all felt. It was like how you feel after a thorough cleaning of your house, how you want to sit in the room and take a deep breath and just enjoy the cleanness and lack of clutter."

Holly did more than enjoy and admire the monks' simplicity. From years of running her consulting business, she knew how clearing clutter can free the mind, even enhance creativity. When she returned home from the monastery, she told me, "I had a strong urge to re-create that atmosphere in my house." She resolved to take action in a practical way: "My husband and I sold or gave away much of the furniture that was crowding our space. We're down to a couch, chair, stereo, and plants in our living room. The room feels wonderfully free and open. Our friends comment on how airy and spacious it seems. And it takes less time to clean! I'm discovering great joy in this."

Letting go of what we don't need can allow us to open our lives to small, uncluttered blessings: The forest's scent of pine. The riot of yellow on a kitchen counter from daffodils picked from the yard. Limbs strong enough to walk or run on. Food enough to eat and share with friends at a party. All these things do not require a bulging bank account. Sometimes, when seen in the right light, what we already have is very great indeed. Explains one woman, "I thought of my constant conversations with myself about wanting a new couch, a weekend cottage, a bigger house on a quiet street and realized my discontent was cheating me of the life I had."[8] But it need not. Not when we turn our eyes to little things that can mean much.

When I look at things through a single eye, through a soul that finds rest in God, I receive my toast in the morning, a bowl of cereal, a cup of tea as a gift from God. I enjoy a movie, even if it isn't at the poshest theater on opening night. I am more inclined to own things without possessing them. Without being possessed by them. "Possession is an obsession in our culture," writes Richard Foster. "If we own it we feel that we can control it; and if we control it, we feel that it will give us more pleasure. The idea is an illusion."[9] It is possible to enjoy something *more* when we realize it as a gift, not a given. One single, rich piece of chocolate enjoyed with a friend satisfies more than handfuls of M&Ms eaten on the run. The small, savored and noticed, fills us more than the merely ostentatious ever could. We can even enjoy something in *giving it away,* seeing the pleasure it gives another.

LEARN TO LIVE WITH MORE TRUST, LESS ANXIOUS CONTROL

To think about simplifying does demand of us a more radical trust. Dorothy Day, tireless worker for the poor, talked about our need to embrace what she called "precarity," a willingness not to live only by the dicta of financial security. In doing so, we find ourselves more dependent on God. More liable not to live as an isolated island of self-sufficiency. More willing to receive the concern and help of others. But to a heart free enough from worry, risks are possible. It is no accident that when Jesus told his followers to "seek first [God's] kingdom and his righteousness," He immediately said, "and all these things [what we eat, drink, wear] will be given to you as well" (Matthew 6:33). Knowing that, I can hold my things with a looser grasp, and sometimes let go altogether. I can stop hedging my bets.

Not long ago I grew concerned about our family's minivan, an aging, rusting car on its last wheels. It wasn't the appearance that worried me; the Plymouth Voyager had long since ceased looking sleek. I was concerned about safety. One morning, standing at my bathroom sink and brushing my teeth, I was praying and felt sudden, specific guidance that it was time to get another car. That's it. Just "It's time." It took us a couple of weeks to act on it, but on the very day we bought another car, even while we were at a used car dealer haggling over a price, the Voyager refused to start when my son went out to take it on an errand.

When I got the car started the next day, I took it for a drive, only to have it slip out of gear with a thud, then lurch forward. The transmission was going. God's timing and direction about the new car seemed providential. And then, within a week, a construction worker building a car from parts for his daughter happened to drive by our house. He saw the old van parked by the side of the house, pulled in our driveway, and offered to buy it on the spot.

Things don't always go so smoothly; I have known panicky, sleep-troubling moments when income seemed as though it would fall far short of expenses. There may be a cost in living with trust. Lack of money may dictate decisions to forgo things I truly want and can easily justify. Simplicity comes with risks that may drive us almost frantically into dependence on God. But I also know that trying to bring my relationship to possessions under the eye of God is ultimately freeing. God is not stingy, but equipped with infinite resources. When I follow that God, generosity becomes an option. Knowing that today will provide the daily bread I need allows me not to exhaust myself in storing up what I think in my worst moments I will need. I leave the issue in hands far bigger—infinitely so—than mine.

Simplicity, after all, is not a grim exercise, but a joyous way to freedom—not a heavy duty, but an invitation to another kind of abundance. We simplify when we organize life around what matters. And especially when we leave the most room possible for the One who alone can simplify—and satisfy.

Chapter 6

EVERYDAY
Rhythms

There is never enough time to do everything, but there is always enough time to do the important.
ANONYMOUS

There is a moment in each day that Satan cannot find.
WILLIAM BLAKE

$\mathcal{N}ot$ long ago an errand to pick up my flu-ridden son's biology homework took me out for a mid-day drive. The mid-September air was warm, the oaks along the rural road a vivid green, the goldenrod out in full force. Because the radio in the van was out, I couldn't click it on as I usually would.

Instead I felt a sudden, exhilarating moment of freedom. Here I was, unencumbered by office responsibilities, a beautiful late-summer morning to myself. It started out to be a routine errand and ended up being an excursion. I felt a wonderful freedom. I even found myself praying while I drove—thanking God for the Tennes-see countryside, for a daughter happy in school, for being able to devote time to writing.

And then I realized, *Part of praying simply has to do with leaving spaces in my life.* I prayed, almost unthinkingly, simply because I had opportunity to do so. If I had been bustling to make an appointment for which I was late, if I had filled my morning with phone calls, crowding out any time for the errand, I might not have prayed. I would have missed the sunshine. The trick was not letting life get so overrun that it doesn't allow thoughts of God to find root and grow.

I wish I could say every day of my life held such pauses. But I know that with all the demands I negotiate each day, I maintain a fragile balance—sometimes a juggling act. Frazzled, frenetic, stressed out as I frequently am, I often feel unfriendly about my relationship to time. Myriad books, tapes, and courses on time management tell me I'm not alone.

When Stephan Rechtschaffen asks participants in his seminars on wellness and time, "Do you have enough time in your life?" he says only one or two out of a class of fifty people say yes. When he asks these few how they feel about life, they tend to give a knowing smile and say they feel great. He writes, "The other 95 percent—like most of us—are experiencing what I call 'time poverty.'" When asked how that feels, they often say things like "Frustrating. Stressful." "Like I can't breathe." Or "Whatever I'm doing, I feel like I should be doing something else."[1]

Again and again my use and abuse of time affects my soul. Rushing from task to task can dull my faculties. Stretching my life to the very edges of the page leaves little margin for reflection and insight. And leaving renewing pauses amid the harried push and hurried pull—that leaves me a different man. But how do I follow my best instincts when so many tasks and demands clamor for attention?

I had a conversation today with an artist and designer, an up-

and-coming professional. She bemoaned her lack of time, her hectic lifestyle. "Our generation," she said, "has lost something by always rushing around." She wistfully mentioned her parents, who for all their hard work, she believed, had a leisure her life lacks. We said to one another, *How ironic.* What generation has seen as many "time-saving" devices as ours? We have microwaves that heat food instantly, e-mail that reaches across the globe in minutes, bread makers that allow one to stay busy (even sleep) while loaves rise and bake. Still, it seems, there are never enough hours in the day. "Lunch hours" become times to entertain business clients. Supper means quick bites squeezed between soccer games and evening meetings. We feel too many pressures and too few spaces. We rarely talk about our time in terms of life and freedom.

Somehow waking up must bring calm and simple graces and occasional spaces. I have no interest in an approach to the spiritual life that only tightens my time bind and increases pressure on my schedule. What I need is fundamentally to change my relationship to time, to the God of time. John, a colleague, tells me, "Sometimes I get off balance in my schedule, forgetting to leave breathing room. And then I find myself experiencing a deeper level of fatigue." I know what he means. Sometimes I get too driven by the demands of work or household.

But then I look longingly at spiritual sources. Part of me naturally gravitates to the places of prayer and space that nourish me. I recall how Jesus often withdrew to a "solitary place," away from the clangorous demands of others (Mark 1:35). In the center of active ministry and faithful service we find Jesus protecting moments for restful breathing and silent breaks. He refused to let life be consumed by a clattering, constant stream of demands. With my restless heart and chattery mind how can I live more like that? Knowing what my schedule looks like in the hard light of day, how can I weave more awareness of God into my daily activities? And what about finding time to pray and reflect on God in the first place?

Several ways of framing the issue have helped me.

PICTURE A GENTLE RHYTHM, NOT A RIGID AGENDA

I've never been the type to rely heavily on appointment notebooks and day planners. Still, at times I've nobly tried to use devotional time management systems to order a simpler, saner, more spiritual life. I've thought they could hold some key to more quiet times with God. When it has come to the praying itself, I've sometimes turned prayer into a list of agenda items. I've felt as if I've had to consult my watch frequently, making sure I "clocked" adequate time in God's presence. I've mapped out what I would say, how many verses of the Bible I would read, the list of people I would pray for.

I frequently failed to keep the regimens up, ending in a cycle of guilt and unrealized hopes. Some days saw my best intentions swallowed in a sea of toddlers' demands or crises at work. Over the years I've realized how turning my times for reflection on God into an item on my calendar is not enough. Or wrong to start with. Some people, I know, thrive on organizing their lives and charting their activities. They may be able to do the same with living a more spiritually awake life. But I often find another approach more useful, more natural.

I try instead to conceive of my times of prayer and reflection as part of a rhythm. Growing in awareness of God is not about a program, but a Person. DayTimers or Filofaxes can help us manage appointments or social obligations, but they can turn the spiritual life into a mechanical system. "Schedules are wooden, inflexible, static, and impersonal," pastor, teacher, and author Eugene Peterson warns. "Fitting prayer into a schedule is like trying to fit God into a schedule."[2] God doesn't conform so neatly.

If rhythm becomes the guiding image, times to reflect and pray, times spent in spiritual communion with others, will take on another cast. We will be looking at the whole of life, not just "spiritual" activities. The varied ways we live and move and have our being will all have a place. The words *time* and *tide,* I'm told, trace back to a single, ancient language root. They have in common after all these centuries the idea of ebbing and flowing. While the hours of our day march ever onward, they do not move in a dull, unbroken pace. Things come and go. We advance, we retreat. "There is a time for everything," the writer of Ecclesiastes said (3:1, 7), "a time to be silent and a time to speak." Everything has a "season." Which means, in the spiritual life, finding patterns that fit us. We consider our natural alternations: Work and rest. Action and prayer. Intimacy and solitude. We remember how one feeds the other. How one drives us to the other. We move in and out as our lives and our souls require. As we get the feel for the cadence, prayer takes an uncontrived place in our daily activities. Teachers of poetry know how important rhythm is to poetic language. Nursery rhymes, for instance, not only rhyme, they hook the reader with their rhythm, carry one along on the lilt of their accents and quiet syllables. There is something engaging, soothing, in the rhythm. We learn to fall in with it. So also we learn the rhythms of relationship with God. We start with our lives as they are and look for ways spiritual aspiration and daily duties can find their proper places.

In this view, time is not something we control. Nor is God's work in the world, which through prayer and worship we try to join. What God is orchestrating through our lives is more like a dance than a lockstep. "In his heart a man plans his course," goes the proverb, "but the Lord determines his steps" (Proverbs 16:9). Sometimes the most profound moments in our relating to God happen when we get out of the way. We just take off our shoes and realize we are standing on holy ground. And often our crying need for God, when we listen to it, will keep us on our knees before God. "I come to God every morning," says my wife, who frequently leaves her calendar in her desk, unopened, "because I desperately need God, not because it's an appointment. I can't go through life without what I gain in those times I spend in His presence." We pray about our praying, and let God open up natural spaces in which we can seek Him. And then let God lead us from the mountaintop down to the valley where we resume our daily commitments.

And with rhythm as our working image rather than rigid assignments, we begin to watch for pauses, even in the busiest day, to take a deep breath and remember God's goodness. To join in what God is already about. "It is well," writes Teresa of Avila, "to seek greater solitude so as to make room for the Lord and allow His Majesty to do His own work in us."[3] And it is "well" to take a coffee break with a colleague and do more than discuss work. A walk around the building mid-afternoon can refresh, even if we cannot steal away to a church or retreat house.

Music is beautiful not only for its notes but also its pauses; percussion gives rhythm only with the alternation of sound and silence. So with our days. Our breakfast conversations and work meetings and evening phone calls will have more depth and focus when we have not made the morning a blur. It helps to remember that sometimes. Doing so encourages us to invite God into spaces we leave open or, in delighted surprise, find open before us, much as happened on my mid-day errand when I went to pick up my son's homework.

And if we cannot manage time each day to pray formally, we can think about the whole week, unearthing spaces for prayer in that longer frame. When I was having trouble with regular morning prayer times, a spiritual advisor once suggested I look for "pools of prime time" in each week—an evening here, a Sunday afternoon there. That could be my quiet time when individual days could not seem to provide it.

Thinking of the spiritual rhythm within each week also helps me make sense of the Sabbath, a day of rest and worship in several religious traditions. Sabbath literally means "ceasing." Even God rested on the seventh day of the Genesis creation story, the Hebrew Bible says. And if God does, why not us? "Remember the Sabbath day by keeping it holy. Six days you shall labor and do all your work, but the seventh day is a Sabbath to the Lord your God. On it you shall not do any work, neither you, nor your son or daughter, nor your manservant or maidservant, nor your animals, nor the alien within your gates. For in six days the Lord made the heavens and the earth, the sea, and all that is in them, but he rested on the seventh day" (Exodus 20:8–11).

The practice of Sabbath rest came as a fundamental innovation in the history of humankind. Before the Jews, no ancient civilization hallowed a weekly day of rest. No one practiced this weekly re-creation through prayer, worship, and the halting of work. Our culture is the better for it.

In early biblical history, the rhythmic pattern of rest and work went beyond the week, too. It had bearing also on the longer stretches, from which we get our culture's custom of the sabbatical leave for study or renewal. The rhythm of rest and work, time on and time off, so interwove the fabric of daily life that Moses told the farmers of Israel, "For six years you are to sow your fields and harvest the crops, but during the seventh year let the land lie unplowed and unused" (Exodus 23:10–11). Modern agriculture knows the wisdom of letting fields lie "fallow." No field (no life!) can keep producing without being given a chance to rest. A friend of mine who grew up in rural England described the farming like this: "One year a field is planted with wheat, the next, vegetables, then oats. On the fourth year the land is left fallow, and the community's livestock would graze the field, fertilizing the acre-sized fields with their droppings." We need the nutrient-rich droppings that our own fallow times can give. We need vacations not just for our bodies but also for our souls. Holy leisure becomes a kind of ground out of which creativity and more focused work can grow.

Not long ago Kevin Miller, a publishing executive I've known for years, found himself in a soul crisis in the wake of an accident that threw him from a Jet-Ski. Initially, it appeared that Kevin suffered only a minor concussion. But in the weeks after the accident he found himself plagued by bouts of ferocious anxiety. He ended up in the office of a psychiatrist, who identified the problem as adjustment disorder, following the traumatic accident. But the doctor suggested that Kevin's accident wasn't the sole cause of his trouble. He urged Kevin not to rely only on anti-anxiety medications, but to use the occasion to explore some fundamental questions. Doing so, Kevin realized, would take more than emotional leftovers at the end of crammed work days. So he asked his employer for a two-week sabbatical.

Kevin does not find it *easy* to take time off from his deadline-driven management job. He organizes each day with to-do lists. He keeps a neat desk. But he also is trying to find balance. So here he is, even as I write, spending time with no goal except, as he put it, "to lie on my back, look up into heaven, and hope God looks back at me. I want to walk the wooded path near my home and feel dry fall leaves rustle against my feet. I want time simply to think and *be*." Already he is confronting his idolizing of his intellect, a perfectionism that drives him to achieve, an inordinate need for others' approval. Only in the rhythm of intense engagement with work and deliberate withdrawal from work will Kevin find what his soul needs. I do not need quite such a drastic measure, not now, but I do need to take times for life-giving, soul-refreshing breaks. Every now and then I need a weekend retreat at a monastery or a few days of vacation with my family. These are not the extravagances of a spoiled life. They are essentials for a balanced one.

There is always the danger, of course, of too much rest, too much withdrawal. Who hasn't known people who use religion as an unhealthy refuge? Some flit from spiritual conference to spiritual conference, always questing for a new spiritual buzz. But for most of us, the temptation lures from the other pole. "I'm forever working on learning to 'be still and know that [He is] God,' " says my friend Louise, echoing the verse from the Psalms. "I'm trying to discipline myself to be still, to be in the receptive mode rather than the 'go get it mode.' I think God's presence comes to us but often we dash off to the next urgent thing before we realize God is there. We can miss so much by demanding that God live by our human schedule rather than us adapt to His timing."

And so I try not to make each day a stream of nonstop activity. Some mornings I manage to go running in my neighborhood before the day runs away with me. Other times I sit quietly with my wife, lingering over coffee after supper, after the kids have eaten and gone off with friends to play. And I try to pray, in the morning, through the day, even at night as my eyelids grow heavy and I drift off.

FRAME THE DAY WITH PRAYER
AND SPIRITUAL REFLECTION

If rhythm implies gentle alternations natural to growth, it does not mean there is never order. While some things in life seem to happen naturally, effortlessly, many things happen because we deem them important enough to ensure that they happen. We enlist the will. For truly big projects, of which building a life of prayer is one, you cannot do without some deliberateness. "The truth is that we only learn to pray all the time everywhere after we have resolutely set about praying some of the time somewhere."[4] I have a friend, a busy, sometimes overcommitted freelance writer, who decided she would sit down to write only after she had spent a half-hour in prayer. She doesn't see it as a stunning, overblown regimen, and her resolve is not for everyone, but it keeps her praying. It keeps her connected. It's her way to stay in rhythm.

The temptation I fall into, particularly when busy or stressed, is to plow into the things I think need to be done. But sometimes I need to participate in the holy waste of giving fifteen minutes, maybe more, asking for God's help, trusting that He has resources I don't. And those times consciously spent in the presence of God—morning or evening, for an hour or a few quick minutes—become some of the most significant times of my day. They allow me to reconnect to God and regain my inner bearings. The effects that ripple throughout my daily life keep me coming back. And often I have found my early morning times of prayer becoming a habit. I don't even think about whether I should or can. The pull of habit assumes I will. I feel out of sync when I miss them.

These times for prayer are never elaborate; I use my prayer rope to keep my mind on my repetitions of a short prayer, I read from the Psalms, sometimes from *The Book of Common Prayer*. I try to pray about the day ahead. And I pray for people I've promised to pray for. I also just try to sit still. Sometimes that is the great accomplishment. In a recent Gallup Poll, 64 percent of respondents, when asked how they prayed, said that they "sit quietly and just think about God." Not a bad definition of spiritual practice.

I find it helpful to try to do this at the beginning of the day, sitting quietly in the living room. I know others wouldn't dream of attempting such a thing in the morning, at least not before a stiff cup of coffee. But whenever, wherever, even a small chunk of time can keep the soul alive.

And I make it a point to read the Bible every day, if I can, even if it turns out to be no more than a psalm or a few verses. I have found its tested truth too vital to neglect. John Mogabgab understands it like this: "Becoming familiar with God's patterns of self-disclosure in the Bible and other spiritual-life writers," he said, "helps me discern God's ways of moving now." I can't figure out my soul's longings by myself. I need recourse to God's revealed truths.

And not only the Bible. Sometimes I read a spiritually oriented book to supplement the verses from the Bible. This requires a bit of concentration; I love books and delight in them. Every kind—novels, short stories, memoirs, even how-to books—draws me. But I also know that some books merely entertain me (a valid enough function) while others enlarge me. It's the latter I try to use for my prayer times. Thomas Merton explains that books (he might have said magazines, too) can speak to us like God, another human voice, or the noise of the city we live in: "They speak to us like the noise of the city when they hold us captive by a weariness that tells us nothing, give us no peace, and no support, nothing to remember, and yet will not let us escape." But they speak to us like God "when they bring us light and peace and fill us with silence."[5] That kind of reading fills the soul and enriches the day.

I understand that the novelist Flannery O'Connor, after washing her face and brushing her teeth each night, would read a couple of pages of medieval theologian Thomas Aquinas, to, as she put it, "give my mind a good scrubbing." Which reminds me, challenges me, to think about how spiritual reflection can frame my day—front and back, opening *and* closing. Reflection on God can help me put the day to bed, so to speak. Usually my nighttime pattern is to read until my eyes grow heavy. It's typically a novel or memoir. But the other night I did something different, something I want to do more of. Rather than losing myself in my latest book, I simply rested my head on the pillows, my eyes scanning our still-lit bedroom, and I prayerfully considered the day. I gave it back to God. I recalled a simple verse of Psalms. And I took in the beauty of our room, thanking God for His good gifts.

I once heard of an elderly woman who was ill. The late African-American pastor and essayist Howard Thurman told her story.

Each morning when she awoke she said the phrase, drawn from the Psalms, "This is the day that the Lord has made. I will be glad and rejoice in it." At night she repeated her phrase, but because "rejoice" and "be glad" are not very restful words, she said, "This is the night the Lord has made. I will relax and rest in it." One day she fell, but managed to pull herself up. Shaken and in pain, she got into bed and pulled up the covers. As she turned out the light she said, "This is the night the Lord has made. I will relax and cry in it."

Realizing with a start what she had said, she mingled her laughter with her tears, her joy with her prayers.[6] She had framed her day beautifully.

FILL TIME WITH LITTLE REMINDERS
AND SMALL GESTURES

Recently I spent a weekend in a monastery in the hills of Kentucky. The Abbey of Gethsemani is renowned for its emphasis on prayerful silence. I knew also that the late Thomas Merton, whose writings on spirituality and social causes made him a publishing phenomenon for decades, had lived there. I wanted to experience firsthand the life I had read about in Merton's journals. I wanted a taste of the monks' quiet holiness.

That weekend I prayed with the monks during their regular "office" of prayers, stumbling into the church at designated hours throughout the day (and night, when I could manage it). Never will I forget the resonant, other-worldly melodies of their plainsong chants reverberating within the abbey church's whitewashed walls. During the day I walked the woodland "knobs" of the hundreds of acres surrounding the compound. I read. I prayed. I soaked in the wondrously sacred atmosphere. I worried about nothing but gently seeking God and God's rest.

And I came back home more alive than I had felt for months, maybe years. In the days that followed, I would awaken in the wee hours and want to keep warm the spiritual glow that surrounded that weekend. It was wonderful, and I will never forget it.

But I also know that I cannot spend every weekend at Geth-semani. I cannot get far without tending to the everyday stuff—the weekly patterns, the daily responsibilities, the momentary disciplines. The way I spend my day as I make breakfast, edit a book, help my son with his homework, turn out my bedside light, *these* things matter in my spiritual growth. So I try to stay alert for God's fingerprints on the everyday matters.

For a time I tried to make it a point that when I got into the office that the act of punching the on button on my computer would be a signal for prayer. I didn't always remember, but I tried to let the minute while my computer booted up become a pause of prayerful waiting. One friend tells me, "I make the early morning time, when I'm struggling to open my eyes and pull myself out of bed, a time for intercessory prayer. I pray for the situations and people I expect to face during the day. Then, as I prepare my shower, I try to see it as a symbol of cleansing, the showering of God's grace in our lives. And I try always to thank God for food before I enjoy it."

So it is with household duties, professional work, social obligations, friendly visits, leisure pursuits—all these and more we turn into moments for God. In the corners and longer stretches of each day and week we link them to God's great work. Time then achieves another dimension. Touches of a great Presence make the "ordinary time" a season for the sacred, all the time, even when I forget to notice and need to be carried along by grace, by others' prayers. Even when I convince myself I'm too busy to pray.

TRUST THAT THERE WILL BE TIME ENOUGH

The biggest issue in my finding time to pray is not where to put it in my schedule. It's believing that there will be time in the first place to make it possible. To spend any time praying means believing that

God has created a day in which there is sufficient time to do what He wills. Perhaps not everything I think of to do, but at least what is necessary, what God needs doing. On the first day, we read in Genesis, God created the day. Was it a defective day? At the end of each day of God's creating, He called what He had made "good." Did what He make somehow lack what it needed?

Sometimes when my schedule seems impossible I will confide my stress and anxiety to my wife. She will remind me, gently chide me, "God doesn't run out of hours. If God promises to provide all you need, that includes all the *time* you need." When we confidently pray, as Jesus taught us, "Give us this day our daily bread" we can also pray, "Give us this day the time we need."

And sometimes time surprises us. This morning I thought I faced an either/or choice: to sit at my desk and work or to give my body some needed exercise and go running. I decided to run—to enjoy the fresh scent after the night's rain, to opt for long-term health instead of the short-term deadline. What I didn't realize was how in this case it wasn't an either/or at all: while I jogged, ideas for my project flooded my mind. I felt refreshed, recharged, able to assume my work with redoubled focus. What seems humanly impossible sometimes gently works itself out. Someone is late for an appointment, giving us an unexpected breather between meetings. A meeting we couldn't seem to squeeze in but "had to" attend gets canceled. Even waiting to pick up a child from a ball practice may give us a sudden, unexpected space for conversation with someone we needed to catch up with and comfort. We discover little graces in the schedule.

It is the same when thinking about spending time in concentrated prayer or meditation. We assume we cannot afford to pause. To read a book that feeds the soul. To attend a morning prayer or chapel service. I remember a difficult time when I worked for a publishing company and faced impossible deadlines. Then, at the last hour, a legal issue on a book we were rushing to press gave me insomnia: not at night, when I would drop into bed exhausted, but in the predawn hours, when I would awaken with an agitated digestive tract, unable to drift back to sleep, too tired to get up. I would rehearse the outcomes, dreading the possibilities. But I also remember praying. Desperate, grasping prayer, yes. But I found stress not only a discomfort but a motivator. I found myself turning to God for dear life. And I found resources I could never have invented. I learned how prayer could be woven into even the most stressful, demanding times. God provided a way.

Perhaps a job that has you to work at dawn makes it impractical for you to pray every morning. Your boss won't let you slow down. Perhaps your toddlers' erratic sleep patterns rouse you and confound your best intentions. You can't even count on their taking regular afternoon naps. The answer is not to give up, but to remember that God is sure to come along to help. Perhaps God has an answer for the long haul you don't see right now: a change of job, a new assignment at the office, a downsizing of your volunteer involvement. You might even feel nudged to change your financial commitments, simplifying your schedule. Or, to your surprise, right where you are, in exactly the life you lead now, God will open up spaces of time you didn't count on, couldn't have orchestrated yourself.

As my alarm jolted me awake early one morning, I recalled a dream from the night: I was driving home in our aging Plymouth Voyager, south on Nolensville Road, a semirural stretch of highway leading from Nashville. I knew I was low on gas. It was very dark outside, just before dawn. And all of a sudden the headlights went out. The motor died. I had run the gas tank dry. But I was able, just barely, to coast into a convenience market with a couple of gas pumps. I pulled next to the gas pumps just as the car finally stopped. I had had precisely enough gas to carry me here. Next I saw out of my rearview mirror an attendant already pumping the car full of gas! I had unwittingly steered into the full-serve island.

As I came fully awake from my dream, I realized how eager I was to get to my spot on the couch in the living room for my prayer time. Once there, I drew in a deep breath. I sensed that God would come and meet me. I had run out of inner fuel, my dream told me, but God was eager to fill me, not with nice thoughts, but with a gracious presence—God Himself.

Chapter 7

Waking Up

TO MORE
THAN A JOB

When work is soulless, life stifles and dies.
ALBERT CAMUS

What I really lack is to be clear in my mind what I am to do, not what I am to know. . . . The thing is to understand myself, to see what God really wishes me to do.
SØREN KIERKEGAARD

One November evening some years ago, I sat watching television with my wife and family, snug in the living room of our suburban Houston home. I've forgotten what we watched, but I vividly remember the restlessness that sent me into the crisp night air for a walk.

Once outside I could smell the wood smoke from a neighbor's fireplace. Under the stars, ambling along a sidewalk, I sensed a call. After years of questioning, I felt with sudden certainty that my growing interest in writing was "right." It was as though someone gave me permission to do what I most wanted to do. "I felt something deep in me relax," I later wrote in my journal, "and say yes." There was no audible voice, nothing dramatic save the starry sky, but some deep part of me knew what I was to be about.

I also felt puzzled. Writing seemed impractical. I lacked formal training. My wife and children depended on my income as a pastor and I knew that even established writers struggle to make a living wage. I worried, feeling the pull but not seeing the possibilities. When I told the editor of a publication I wrote for that I wanted to be a writer, he suddenly acted nervous. "Listen," he warned. "The folks I know who live off their writing income are starving." I had desire and direction, but little clue how to get where I seemed pointed.

Slowly, I began finding my way. My call seemed less and less an out-of-reach dream. I wrote magazine articles in the evenings and a reasonably encouraging number got accepted and published. Soon I was writing a college centennial history book on a half-time, paying arrangement. I moved on to work as an editor on a magazine staff. And in my late thirties, I became an editor for a book publisher. I wasn't writing on the job then, really. But each day had me working with manuscripts, rubbing shoulders with writers, learning the trade. And in the margins of my free time I was managing to write books, feeling more capable with each one. On my fortieth birthday, I found myself reading a book with the promising title *To Build the Life You Want, Create the Work You Love*. Based on what you know you enjoy, the author said, dream about what your working day could look like. She encouraged people to listen deeply. And begin taking concrete steps.[1] Maybe you can make your job more than you thought, she said. Perhaps what you really want to do can be done. I sensed she was right. I was growing more and more confident that my calling was finding its place in the concrete realities of my life.

Now I devote many of my working hours to writing. A kind of dream has come true, at least for now. I get impatient for my books to attract more attention. I worry about whether there will be a constant stream of projects. And with a wife working outside the home, I now juggle new family responsibilities, including primary responsibility for home schooling our middle child. But I take delight in watching a calling unfold. For now, I'm doing what I am made to do.

Whatever the job, wherever the workplace, as the soul awakes it may see work in a new light. No longer will we want to go through the motions or just show up. Because we spend as much as half of the hours of each day on the job[2], we long for something that not only puts food on the table but helps us feel productive. That gives a sense of purpose. We search, says Frederick Buechner, "for a self to be, for other selves to love, and for work to do."[3] I know I want to see more at the end of the day than a paycheck or a pile of folded laundry. I want to see my efforts "fit" into a larger scheme. So we ask, Can work not only feed the body but nourish the soul? Can it enrich all of life—not just the checking account? And how do we make the best of the sometimes awkward wait between the call and the realization? As we live and work in between the ideal and the reality, as we sometimes must, how do we nurture a spiritual life?

We are not often encouraged in our culture to ask the larger questions about work. It's assumed that salary and prestige and rank provide all we need to stay satisfied. Something in us knows better.

If God made work part of the order of creation, it must be possible to do ours without sacrificing our souls. But how?

TURN WORK INTO A PLACE FOR WAKEFULNESS

When I think of the varied jobs I've had, from bagging groceries to earn money for college to preaching sermons every Sunday as a pastor, I realize that work of almost any kind—at home, classroom, office, factory, hospital, on the road—can provide opportunities for growth. Even jobs that burden with monotony and bury with mundane details can give the soul lessons.

I write this afternoon to the revving background noises of chain saws and a gas-powered wood chipper. A crew of four men is removing a huge elm placed awkwardly by our front porch. For a few moments I watched while their leader carefully sawed a wedge on the side he wanted the tree to fall on. Then he sliced through the opposite side, his saw blade moving to meet the cut-out wedge. As planned, the tree began to creak, tip, and fall, aided by coworkers pulling the roped tree to where they wanted it to fall. I began thinking about what their job must be like. I thought of the sheer physical fatigue they must feel, some days the drudgery. But I also observed how close they were to the rough bark, the soil from which the trees grew. All the while they have pushed themselves, almost scurrying. Now, with the tree down, with the branches lopped off and chipped, the sawdust and stray twigs raked up, I saw them all visibly relax. A couple took out cigarettes. I doubt if they spoke much of God or of the created order amid which they walked and pulled and grunted. But you could almost hear them giving a sigh of relief for a job well done. They seemed satisfied.

Must such work be any less a place for the soul to wake up than writing books, preaching sermons, or running a homeless shelter? I find an answer by thinking about Jesus. He worked in a carpenter's shop for most of His life, and surely those days were not wasted, surely He "lived out" His relationship with His divine Father there. And He must have done very physical work. A spurious group of stories about Jesus known as the Gospel of Thomas, circulated in the ancient world, describing an ethereal, wonder-working child Jesus, who miraculously lengthened mismatched planks during jobs at His father's carpentry shop. But Thomas's Gospel was eventually repudiated as heretical. Jesus' earthly life was not a mere shell or disguise. He grew up with all the resinous smells of cut wood, with the texture of grain, even the occasional splinter stuck in the finger. He was God, but God in the flesh. Work allowed Him to take His calling into the same kinds of scenes and circumstances we face.

That model reminds us that it is in the daily round of doing our work that we pursue the simple, the lasting, the good. And even the hard and stretching times at work, the stresses and setbacks, can become occasions to wake up.

A unique characteristic of work makes this so: We choose our friends or mate, but perhaps in more than any other setting, in work we live alongside people we have not chosen. This motley assortment—some we naturally like, others we can barely stand—come with the job. They may have political outlooks that grate. They may demand too much. They may ridicule our beliefs. Which means we may find ourselves stretched. The everyday grist of it—hallway conversations, the relief of a project finally put in the mail, completed, the hard and gritty details—requires of us growth we might not otherwise experience. And that is good. "Drudgery is one of the finest touchstones of character there is," wrote Oswald Chambers. "Drudgery is work that is very far removed from anything to do with the ideal—the utterly mean grubby things; and when we come in contact with them we know instantly whether or not we are we are spiritually real."[4] Sometimes financial obligations offer us no choice but to show up at eight every morning. Over the years, I have worked at jobs filled with stresses, pressures, even goals I did not share. We work in jobs that do not enlist our creativity, for bosses who care nothing for our "fulfillment." Sometimes we slug away. Sometimes our calling comes through tasks others impose on us. We do not live in unlimited freedom.

But even when we seem to limp along with it, dissatisfied and frustrated, work brings good to our souls.

For three years in the mid-1980s, I felt like a combination entrepreneur, evangelist, salesman, administrator, and spiritual guide. My wife, Jill, and I were sent to gather and organize and build a new church in the suburbs of Houston. An organization of churches funded our efforts, even buying a plot of choice real estate next to a YMCA for our future church building. Friends told us, "If anybody can make this project work, it's you two." With pride in our creative plans, we pulled up our U-Haul into the driveway of our new suburban Houston house, full of hope.

Soon after our arrival, Houston's economy collapsed. Families we attracted to our congregation lost jobs and moved out of state. We continued publicizing our congregation and attracted a healthy stream of visitors and inquirers; we worked hard and long. But despite all our labors, before many months we braced ourselves for failure. We had the difficult task of informing our supporters and financial backers that the young church was failing. All our hard work seemed for naught.

I often went jogging in the early mornings to get perspective and pray. During one morning run, I heard a summons. "I want you to die to your plans, your ambitions for this church," it said. The words were freeing while painful. When it became more and more clear that our church-planting venture might never succeed, I wrote often in my journal of feeling discouraged and "closed in." Thoughts of work left me unsettled. It was the hardest job I've tackled.

Jill and I eventually resigned our posts. But those three difficult years in Texas opened up profound discoveries about ourselves. I learned some things about my strengths—and weaknesses. I found myself praying more. And I opened my career plans to God in a way I had never done before. I have never in my life felt so professionally restless, yet probably never grew so much, in every way. For all its difficulty, work became a place of growth.

` TALK CALLING, NOT JUST JOB OR DUTY

There is an old story about three people making rocks:

"What are you doing?" asks a passerby.

"Making little rocks out of big ones," says the first worker.

"Earning a living," says the second.

But the third had a longer view: "Building a cathedral."

Sometimes perspective makes all the difference. We tend to reserve lofty terms like *vocation* and *call* to the Billy Grahams and

Mother Teresas. We just hold down jobs. Maybe on the side we do something that truly enriches our lives or others', but work is, well, work.

But a "call" usually isn't dramatic. Often it is simply what is "called for." When we realize that, we can see more clearly how our nine-to-five piece of the puzzle contributes to a larger whole, to a greater end. Some, in the scheme of things, are singled out for notable achievements, for crowds and mass attention. Some work for religious or charitable institutions. But pastors or missionaries or social workers are not the only ones entitled to a sense of purpose in what they earn. The simplest labor is no less special; God eagerly employs all work done with conscience and commitment. He enlists it all into His great purposes. At a conference on seeing work as an opportunity to serve God and people, someone asked a fellow attendee what he did for a living. "I'm an ordained plumber," he replied.

The word *vocation* comes from a Latin word that means to give a bidding or invitation. A vocation is doing what we are invited to do, what is ours to do. It is that simple. Its shape often has to do with our personal talents and our interests, of course. And often what we most enjoy is what we were most clearly made to do. We approach work, then, to do more than finish a job, but to listen to a bidding voice that leads us amid our seemingly little lives. Living by vocation makes us realize that what we do—changing automobile oil or sewing a pair of pants or teaching a classroom of first graders—can always reflect in some way God's intentions. "Every calling is great," said Oliver Wendell Holmes, "when greatly pursued." He might have said, ". . . when *reverently* pursued."

Seen this way, we become God's "partners." Martin Luther, one of the prime movers of the sixteenth-century's Protestant Reformation, argued that not just priest or nun, but milkmaid and black-smith and housewife all shared in God's work in the world. Plowing a field and milking could further God's kingdom and mediate God's presence, he argued, not just worship services in a church. God himself worked, after all, when He created the universe, and thereby made all work holy. And He invites us into holy work, no matter how mundane, when He gives us opportunities to do our jobs.

Even the little is essential to the whole: numbers crunched and forecast to become a budget, dictation turned into crisp letters, seed turned into feed for livestock or green beans for the dinner table. We see beyond the immediate task, to the lives helped, the good done. And that keeps us going.

PAY ATTENTION TO WHAT YOU ENJOY

People often drift into their jobs or careers. The nature of their work has less to do with thoughtful choosing and more to do with a chance meeting with an old friend who gave a lead. Perhaps the wishes (even pressures) of parents pushed one in a certain direction. But many people can be more creative in doing what grows out of their deepest selves.

Sometimes a job or career can be tailored to what we love. This almost always entails risk. When I left full-time pastoral minis-try to join the editorial staff at a magazine, I had to settle for editorial entry-level wages. My family (graciously) paid for my career switch. But I trust I am a better-adjusted father and husband for having done what I needed to do, longed to do. When we live by calling we need not follow the old ideal of staying in one profession for all time. We don't stay locked in by convention or custom. We don't assume we cannot live out our God-given destiny because we must earn a living. An awakened soul tries to hold these two together.

Not long ago I heard consultant Cynthia Tobias on a radio program, talking about her book, *The Way We Work*. She told of working as a paralegal for two years, hardly able to stand what she was doing. The pay provided money she needed, the opportunity was right, and she stayed by sheer force of will. Because of her financial needs, she said, "I knew I would have to do a job that I hated, that had many aspects to it that did not match me." So violent was her reaction to what she had to do, she said, she was physically ill almost every day. "You can do whatever you need to do when you need to do it, for a while," she said. But if it takes every ounce of strength and energy to be something you are not, by the time you get home you will be drained. You will have nothing left. In a prolonged mismatch, she said, you will "create" a catastrophe, your body or your sanity will stand for only so much internal dissonance.[5]

Doing what you enjoy, what God calls you to (often the two are the same), is another matter. I know how energized I can be from an afternoon of productive writing, how drained from a couple of hours of working on a budget or managing production details on a print run. To feel like your strengths are being used and valued, to believe what you are doing fits into larger goals for your life, that can satisfy the soul. It makes sanctified sense. So you ask yourself, "What am I doing when I'm happiest, most successful?" Not to indulge your whims, but so that you open the door to becoming more the person God created you to be.

I recently reread my journals from those years of struggle in

Houston, when we saw our years of work fall apart. I saw again how time after time I struggled with disappointment. But I also detected a deeper undercurrent. What happened around me made me question not only my day-to-day work, but where my life was leading. I recorded the exhilaration I felt one night staying up late finishing an assignment for a magazine for which I wrote a monthly column. It is no accident that my calling to write crystallized during those painful years.

And I noticed that at the time I read an article by the novelist E. L. Doctorow. The reporter asked Doctorow if he liked writing, really liked it. Doctorow nodded: "It's when I'm most myself. When I don't work for a while, for one reason or another, I begin to feel deprived in the way that sleepers feel when they can't dream."

A word often used in conjunction with *call* is *discernment*. It comes from a Latin root which means "to separate" or "to sort out." Because we live amid many voices, within and without, we cannot do without discernment. We have to distinguish the true from the false: What is the voice of conscience and merely the voice of career ambition? Does what we think we hear come from God or from a fantasizing ego? So we pray for discernment. We take tentative steps, praying all the while. We give our sense of direction time to ripen. We test what we want to do against the canons of sound faith and practice. We spend a weekend at a retreat center to think and determine our deepest wishes. "The truth," someone wrote, "depends on a walk around the lake, a stopping to watch a definition growing certain, and a wait within that certainty."

And we turn to others. We are not to figure out our directions or our staying put solo. Discernment is a corporate affair. We test our leanings and leading with friends, with wise teachers, with pastors, with loved ones. They may save us from harebrained schemes. Or give us the resolve to do something courageous. Right now I find myself considering reentry into pastoral and priestly ministry, even while I continue to write. I want now to link the life of the pastor with the work of the writer in ways I have yet to forge. But I also know I need the confirmation or refinement of others. I will turn frequently to trusted friends to ensure that what seems like God's leading is not my vain imagining.

Amid such carefulness is a place for a kind of consecrated, wild winsomeness. We are sometimes tempted to think pursuing a vocation is not for responsible adults. We measure our work by the standards of what some call the American Dream, not by whether we find worth or joy in what we do. Living by vocation rather than the career track may not look prudent. It may have us driving an older car, inhabiting a smaller house or apartment. But the financial sacrifices might be worth the soul's gain. The greatest risk is to end up not doing what God made us to do. Creatively following a call carries its own satisfaction. I want to remember that, and continue to listen to the summoning voice, above and within, wherever it leads.

CONCENTRATE ON WORK,
BUT MAKE ROOM FOR GOD

We spend too much time at work for it not to be a setting for daily seeking and experiencing God. I think of John Mogabgab. One afternoon I ran into him at a hallway outside my office while he rushed to a meeting, one of many in his editorial-management job. He had a notebook and budgets and proposals tucked under his arm. Yet for all his hurry, John exuded a sense of prayerful calm. I asked him about it one day. "I pray to see God in the facts of the budget," he told me. "I'm constantly looking for signs of God's presence." He must somehow find them.

Too often we divorce our "work life" from our innermost beliefs. But to do so is to miss an opportunity to allow a substantial part of our lives to become a place for living with God. Jean-Pierre de Caussade writes of "the vast expanse of the divine will which is eternally present in the shadows of the most ordinary toil and suffering; and it is in these shadows that God hides the hand which supports and upholds us."[6] We forfeit much when we fail to look for that divine hand, even on the job.

Perhaps it is no accident that books on combining work and spirituality now hit the best-seller lists. One finds titles like *The Reflective Executive* or *The Soul of Business.* Managers at corporations—some of them household names—attend seminars on fostering leadership through spiritual values. If spirituality was once a taboo subject in the workplace, it now seems to be trendy. People seem to sense that whatever they do, however involved their concentration, whether they find work fulfilling or not, they can let the workplace help them cultivate a spiritual life. "I find that a life of little whispered words of adoration, of praise, of prayer, of worship can be breathed all through the day," wrote the Quaker Thomas Kelly. "One can have a very busy day, outwardly speaking, and yet be steadily in the holy Presence."[7] Maintaining a spiritual orientation is not easy. It requires vigilance and resolve. But why not try?

I know a woman, a children's librarian, who prays about work during her drive to her job (not with her eyes closed!). It's simple, really, but as her mind turns to the day ahead, to the rambunctious children that cluster around her desk, she silently prays, " 'Let the words of my mouth and the meditations of my heart be acceptable in thy sight, O Lord my Rock and my Redeemer.' " "This helps me," she wrote me, "to stay focused during the day."

Once upon a time, an ancient monastic tale goes, a spiritual advisor wanted to encourage a business owner to go through his work with more awareness of God's Spirit. He said to the man, "As the fish perishes on dry land, so you perish when you get entangled in the world. The fish must return to the water and you must return to the Spirit."

And the man became dismayed. "Are you saying that I must give up my business and go into a monastery?" he asked.

Said the elder, "Definitely not. I am telling you to hold on to your business and go into your heart, to work and pay attention to your soul."[8]

Wherever I am, cooking supper, writing at my desk in my bedroom study, driving to the office for my part-time editing job, I am trying to live with more God-consciousness. I try to pray as well as concentrate on the assignment. I want to live out of a longer view that holds all my work life together, from the frazzled details to the calm moments I break for coffee. Or pause to pray.

One morning some months ago I felt hemmed in. My world seemed crowded with deadlines at the office and family responsibilities. I went jogging in a cool, wonderfully bright October morning. I ran into the section of woodland not far from my house where developers are creating a new subdivision. My trail came to a clearing where the next section was going in. Overhead was wonderfully blue sky. I was surrounded by space created out of what had been dense forest growth.

I thought back to the verse from the Psalms I had read that

morning: "You have not handed me over to the enemy but have set my feet in a spacious place" (Psalm 31:8). *This* is what I need, I felt. So I opened my life to this God who promised space. And I felt the Lord saying, "The room you see around you is what I am giving you in your *life*. You feel cramped, backed into a corner. But I will make you able for the tasks you face. I will not hand you over to the grinding, deadening effects of hurried stress. I will make room in your life for all that I call you to." Indeed, in the next moments I felt I heard distinct guidance about a job involvement that was consuming too much of my time. I felt guidance to whittle down my hours on the project, even though it would mean losing significant income. But I gained the courage to resist the expectations of others who wanted me to keep at a job that was not God's best. In the long run, I will be glad.

Chapter 8

Soul
COMPANIONS

Friendship is like a step to raise us to the love and knowledge of God.
AELRED OF RIEVAULX

When I was in junior and senior high school, I played the drums, crashing and clanging out rhythms that made up in volume what they lacked in sophistication. My older brother played an electric guitar and we sometimes joined forces, the raw melodies and bluesy discord of the Rolling Stones and Jimi Hendrix filling our otherwise conservative household. While, like my brother, I was self-taught, I managed to pound out serviceable beats and fills.

Recently, with my teenage son wanting to play, I decided to try drumming again. At my first time behind my son's new drum set, I remembered a fair amount from before, how to use the kick drum pedal, the swishing hi-hat cymbals, the percussive snare drum. But I quickly grew bored with my old rhythms and patterns. What contented me as a fourteen-year-old couldn't cut it for my adult tastes.

That's when I decided to take lessons.

Within minutes of my first session with my teacher, a professional drummer, I found myself holding my sticks with a grip that improved my control. George helped me adjust my posture behind the hi-hats and bass drum. He jotted down notes for new beats. He *showed* me how it's done. Over the months I caught the feel of new rhythms—jazz, Latin, Afro-Cuban. Almost immediately my skills took leaps that would have taken years of experimenting on my own. I had found someone to guide me.

In different ways, what happened in my efforts to make rhythm has been repeated time and again. As I learn the rhythms of faith and prayer, I benefit from the presence and help of others in countless ways. Over the years, a parent, a pastor, a small group, and a church body have helped make me who I am. They have helped me live in ways I could not on my own. There is a richly communal dimension to any soul's awakening.

This morning the television carried an interview with Dr. Dean Ornish, a noted health authority. While for years he stressed the need for low-fat diets and exercise, now he has turned his attention to the health benefits of emotional support. "Nothing," he said, "has such power to impact our health as love and intimacy." One study found people much more likely to succumb to disease and death if they lived alone, isolated. Love and connectedness are powerful healers. To his concern about physical heart problems, Ornish now warns about what he calls "emotional heart disease"—a lonely lack of friends and family. Our hearts were not made for solitary confinement.

And when it comes to waking up spiritually, I see again and again that I am not made to navigate solo. I need companions to nourish the soul. "We do not wish for friends to feed and clothe our bodies," wrote Henry David Thoreau, "but to do [a similar thing] to our spirits." We need our efforts and aspirations rooted in a community of faith and worship and service.

Sometimes I hesitate about inviting others into my spiritual life, though. I don't want to impose, for one thing. And I get a little nervous. "When people come together," writes Thomas Merton, "there is always some kind of presence, even the kind that can give a person an ulcer."[1] I don't want some well-meaning reformer crashing into my life determined to "fix" me, to fill me full of opinions and directives. And I know how our friendships and ties to larger communities sometimes do not work out. Along with the joys, you risk hurt and pain. Friendships, even when they do not end in conflict, sometimes wane as people drift apart. We create ambivalent bonds. Sometimes I hold back to protect myself.

And the image of the rugged individualist tugs at me, as it does most people in our culture. Our pictures of "together" people tell us we don't really need deep friendships or groups to belong to. We get the idea growing up, like essayist Gerald Early, that needing others points to a kind of weakness: "I felt embarrassed by friendship as a sign that I was not sufficiently self-reliant."[2] We sometimes like the pride and freedom of the child saying, "I did it all by myself." And we feel the pull of do-it-yourselfism strongly when it comes to prayer or knowing God. We don't want to suggest by our emotional neediness that somehow religious faith fails us, that it cannot heal our ills in and of itself. So sometimes we limp along, our vague isolation masked by schedules that make our lives a blur, our inner emptiness covered over by addictions and superficial pleasures. We settle for surface relationships that ultimately do not renew us. Until a crisis jars us, and we finally call a pastor or neglected friend or turn to family.

Even when no crisis looms or no grief needs a crying shoulder, companions in faith help keep me awake. The things they say refresh me when I get discouraged about my praying. Their counsel guides me. Their view of God revives mine when my vision gets narrow. And I need others with whom I can talk and pray and worship. Without the presence and spiritual nurture of others, my life with God suffers. Friendship is an underestimated resource for spiritual life, writes Eugene Peterson, "every bit as significant as prayer and fasting. Like the sacramental use of water and bread and wine, friendship takes what's common in human experience and turns it into something holy."[3] So do the many other ways we participate in a church body. They mediate grace.

Not that I'm all that great at cultivating this fellowship of the soul. Day in and day out I spend time with dozens of people but learn from their lives only haphazardly. Every now and then I will meet with someone over lunch or coffee and talk about things that matter. That helps. But I find it easy not to invest much. "I have a lot of friends," one man confessed, who like me, was in his early forties. "But lately some of them bore me. Maybe it's a mid-life crisis that's making me reassess the people in my life. All I know is, not one is quite like the best friend I had when I was twelve. Come to think of it, I can't say I've ever had a really close friend as an adult."[4] Many of us must confess we have few people we turn to for prayer or help with spiritual questions.

When I'm honest, though, I admit that I'm sometimes lonely. My busy schedule can leave me feeling isolated. I have work colleagues, acquaintances who share my interest in music, neighbors I greet with a wave and smile, even people at church who share my interest in prayer. I have a wife and children who surround life with richness and love. But often I need to go broader and deeper. When it comes to the spiritual dimension, I need what only close sharing with a friend or soul partner or small group can bring. I don't *really* want to do this alone. And I can't. Nor can I be my own pastor, priest, and prophet. I need friends, mentors, and true community. I can get by with the customary slight intimacies, contenting myself with only occasional deep sharing, but more is possible. I realize now that I will not go far if I don't make more room for companions for the soul, for a community of corporate worship.

Sometimes I think about friends I've had over the years. There was my best friend, Don. All through junior high school, he and I could talk about grades, girls, our changing bodies, and our dreams for the future. Every day we walked part of the way home from school together before our streets diverged. He was the son of a Polish Jewish mother and a Mexican Catholic father. To no one's surprise, including his own, he was searching. We had fascinating discussions about what we believed about God, helping each other in the process. I moved away just before high school and never talked with Don again. But then in high school there was Brandt, a bearded countercultural Christian, already in his twenties, who adopted our campus as a kind of mission field. He invited me to meet him at a restaurant once a week to talk about the Bible. Over Cokes or pieces of pie, he helped me apply my faith to daily decisions. How often should I pray? What did I want to do with my life? How should a teenager relate to his parents? He gave moral support as my call to work in a church crystallized, and he influenced the way I approach the Bible to this day.

There have been others, coworkers I've met with semiregularly, sometimes over coffee or pizza; sometimes conversation took a spiritual turn. I carry on a friendship over the Internet with a fellow writer, Chris. Sometimes our e-mail letters make all the difference when my vision for writing flags. Chris called me Christmas Eve, on a day when I was laboring over a manuscript even though it was a holiday, and our conversation lifted my spirits, helped me keep writing. And there have been myriad congregations, places that have ushered me into the presence of God through word, prayer, and sacrament.

And then there has been Kevin. Years ago we discovered the great value of spiritual friendship, a kind of mutual mentoring of the soul.

Kevin had overheard two men discussing how they had each had a friend with whom they talked about spiritual issues. "I began to wonder," Kevin told me, "if I could find that one person in fifty who could listen to my soul." He began to pray simply, "Lord, bring along that kind of person."

Around the time Kevin began praying, I joined the company where he worked. And I felt stirrings similar to his. I wanted the same support that Brandt had given when I met with him weekly in high school, the kind that I had found in a handful of others since. As Kevin and I got to know each other, bumping into each other in the hallways, seeing each other at company functions, we discovered a lot in common—we were close in age, had young children, seemed to view the world similarly. We had the experience that C. S. Lewis describes, where he explains that friendship grows out of a shared interest: "the typical expression of opening Friendship would be something like, 'What? You too? I thought I was the only one.' "[5] We not only felt we had things in common, we thought we could be of real help to one another. We decided to give it a try and meet regularly.

When I first began meeting with Kevin for conversation and prayer, I wasn't sure what to expect. I knew that I wanted someone to talk to about the things that excited or disappointed me. I knew that I longed for more support for my efforts to live a spiritual life. I also knew how often I walked through daily circumstances only partly aware of what was happening, only dimly seeing God's hand in everyday turns of events. I suspected a companion in the Spirit could listen and pray with me. Could help me see something I would otherwise miss. Could help me stay awake when I was tempted to get drowsy.

And I was right. For five years, before I moved out of state, Kevin and I took a lunch hour once a week to share our stresses, anxieties, joys, even doubts. We simply shut the door and met in his office. We gave encouragement, prodded one another to new ways of thinking, and prayed aloud for each other before we broke. Mostly we helped each other listen to what God was saying through the raw material of the routines and milestones of our lives. I have yet, three years after moving away to another state, to find a friendship as deep and inspiring. But I haven't stopped looking, staying open. Most of the time I think I'm remiss in not trying harder. But I know what I'm missing through what I gained, and I trust I will find it again.

Thinking about that companionship makes me think about ways others can help the soul awaken. It makes me think about what can happen when we refuse to limit our conversations to sports or promotions or the latest political controversy. I want to take more risks to join my simple human need for companionship with my soul's need for fellowship and communion with others.

Here are the imperatives for doing so:

RECOGNIZE YOUR NEED
FOR COMPANIONSHIP

Often we simply need someone with whom we can simply *be*. A friend, a family circle, a church can help us face the week's hurts and hopes with the assurance that others know about what we face. We need to know we are not alone.

Some years ago, I discovered how pervasive this longing. For three difficult years in Texas, my wife and I pastored a new church that seemed never to get fully off the ground, as I mentioned earlier. We had arrived with high hopes that the fledgling congregation we were sent to establish would become a thriving church. To our pain and disappointment, it was not to be. My neighbor Joe, a construction contractor and a husky man ten years my senior, became a lifeline. I still remember him walking up to the front door every Monday at 7 A.M., the steaming coffee cup in hand. In my home office, we would work our way through a book of the Bible, each taking turns leading the discussion. I know we took nourishment from the verses we discussed, but what I most remember, not quite ten years later, was the way we shared from our daily lives at the end of each hour before we prayed together. A person who stands patiently by us can make all the difference.

We receive and offer the gift of this support sometimes in small ways, through thoughtful gestures or simple availability. A phone call, an impromptu visit when in the neighborhood, these little kindnesses often are providentially timed and more helpful than we might think. And we don't always have to be physically present to another for us to benefit from another's presence. A man, I'm told, was struggling for truth against fanatical deceit and prejudice in his city. I don't know all the details. But a colleague in a distant city heard of the battle he was waging and sent him a note of encouragement and concern. He told him he cared and was praying for him.

Some years later, when the letter writer had forgotten about the note he sent, a knock came at his door. There stood the man to whom he had written. "I came to thank you," he said. "I had gotten to the place where I thought I was about to have a nervous breakdown, and my wife and I had agreed I should give up the struggle. We were sitting, demoralized, in our living room when I heard the mail being delivered. I went to the mailbox, and there was your note. God wiped the windshield clean, and I started over again."

Another's gentle acceptance and quiet presence can keep us moving patiently, steadily toward a goal. The novelist Jay McInerney once wrote about his former writing teacher, Raymond Carver. McInerney had gone on to become a renowned writer himself and he and Carver, McInerney wrote, were talking about their writing and their careers. McInerney was berating Carver, he said, for going easy on a student who was turning out poor work. In response, McInerney wrote, Carver "told me a story: he had recently been a judge in a prestigious fiction contest. The unanimous winner, whose work has since drawn much praise, turned out to be a former student of his, probably the worst, least promising student he'd had in twenty years. 'What if I had discouraged him?' he said." Concluded McInerney, "As a teacher . . . Carver had a light touch. He did not consider it his job to discourage anyone."[6]

Sometimes the simple act of owning up to something and seeing that the person we tell doesn't drop his or her jaw at our stupidity or weaknesses can give us the courage to keep going. Friends can become bearers of grace. One story about a fourth-century monk (one of those who are often called "desert fathers") shows this: Some old men came to see Abba (Father) Poemen with a question about what to do when desert monastic life wearied their fellow monks. Perhaps, conscious of the rigors of their calling, they expected a stern answer. "When we see brothers who are dozing at [the prayer services]," they asked, "shall we rouse them so that they will be watchful?" Abba Poemen said only, "For my part when I see a brother who is dozing, I put his head on my knees and let him rest."[7]

This quality of simple companionship is worth looking for, worth waiting for. Writer Eugene Peterson tells of a time, when home from his second year of college, he went looking for help. He was spiritually restless, so a friend suggested that Peterson go to see Reuben Lance, a jack-of-all trades, an expert in carpentry, plumbing, masonry—anything manual. Reuben had a certain gruffness about him, and, as Peterson said, he didn't suffer fools gladly. But Peterson went. And what happened was simple, but life changing: "Much of what we talked about was everyday stuff—tools, work, landscape, school. I never had the feeling that he was exploiting my vulnerability in any way. He treated me with dignity. (Twenty-year-old college sophomores aren't used to being treated with dignity.) I felt a large roominess, room to move around, room to be free. He didn't hem me in with questions; he didn't suffocate me with 'concern.' "

Now, looking back, Peterson wonders, "Why do I have so many teachers and helpers, and so few friends who are modest enough and wise enough simply to be companions with me in the becoming and the entering in? In clearing the ground? Removing obstructions? Discerning the presence of God? Listening for the still, small voice?"[8]

The qualities that make for life-changing companionship are

surprisingly simple, doubtless resident in people you already know. Our most helpful friends will usually be ordinary people like us who, because they offer the grace of caring, become extraordinary sources of strength.

GAIN HELP IN LEARNING TO
LISTEN TO LIFE

While many of us look for God in spiritually charged experiences, a wise friend or group can help us wake up amid the everyday realities. They can point out ways that God is at work in our lives. Sometimes we stand too close to our daily frustrations to hear clearly. But soul friends can help us grasp how God is speaking and leading through the ordinary things. I know Kevin—just by being there—often reminded me that the circumstances I would bring up—a frustration at the office, a struggle over vocation, a concern about my impatience with my children—was the setting for the living out of my soul's aspirations. A friend helps us not to forget to listen to deeper intuitions, or to subtler messages of life's events.

Not long ago, on the phone with Kevin (we still call one another every month or two), I mentioned how I was having trouble forgiving someone close to me, who, I felt, had taken advantage of me. I felt cheated. Looking back, I saw some ways I could have kept my friend from unfairly using the situation, and that was making it harder to let go. Kevin saw the issue now was not what had or had not been done (at this point that was beyond everyone's control) but how I was going to process my feelings. "I'm struggling with the need to forgive," I said. "Yet it seems like until I forgive my friend's betrayal this feeling will eat away at me." Kevin rightly confirmed that the time for me to forgive had come. I knew it, but only with another person's simple observation was I able to see and hear clearly that *Yes, that is exactly what I need to do.* He helped me listen to what my life was telling me. My mixed feelings gave way to a clear intention, and I got on with the needed work of forgiveness.

At important moments the perspective of others gives me another set of eyes. He or she or they may see something when my own vision gets cloudy. Sometimes all it takes to stay put in a disheartening situation is a little shift in perspective, as happens to a painter when he moves his easel slightly only to find a whole new landscape panorama. All it takes is another set of ears, straining for the sometimes faint whispers of divine truth gracing daily life.

FIND ENCOURAGEMENT TO WAKE UP TO TRUTH

We live in a highly subjective age, one that flinches at even whispers of moral accountability. We convince ourselves that we can bend the rules, follow our own private interpretations. We battle perennial temptations to "fudge" on ethical choices or cut corners on what really matters. But in our deepest selves, we long to be more than we might be lazily on our own. What the ruler needed, in the children's fable about the emperor with no clothes, was someone, finally, who could break the truth to him. Someone who had the courage to see the emperor in his naked silliness. In a similar way, a friend helps me ground my soul's movements in something more solid than private experience or personal opinion. Not that I need to find a friend who criticizes me and leaves me discouraged. No, just someone who, perhaps by the mere contagion of his or her presence, by model and occasional gentle counsel, helps me keep character a vital concern in my choices.

Sometimes personal ambition blinds me, for example, to what my daily schedule is costing me in stress. Sometimes I cave in too easily to the temptation to neglect what truly matters. Others can help me balance competing demands and bring my choices into harmony with a God-centered way of life. They can help me build the courage that allows me to base my life on something more profound than others' approval. They can question me, perhaps even keep me from drifting into destructive patterns. They can help me stay strong in character areas that sometimes require vigilance, like sexual purity, financial integrity, and family commitments. I may become deceived by sin's subtleties, insensitive to its effects. There are areas where I cannot be completely objective on my own. No wonder a proverb says that he who is his own doctor has a fool for a physician. But companions can help me keep my eyes on God's expectations for my behavior and God's larger purposes for my life.

The late Quaker teacher Douglas Steere tells of hosting the eminent Jewish scholar Martin Buber. Buber was visiting America and scheduled a stop at Haverford College in Pennsylvania, where Steere taught. Steere encouraged Buber to say something at the college's chapel service (what Quakers call a Meeting). Before Buber spoke, the president of the college rose and said what a great thing it was that people could meet each other across barriers of race, nationality, and age. President White had barely finished when Buber rose in his place, looking like a Semitic prophet with his beard and piercing eyes. He looked around and said yes, it was a great thing to transcend barriers. But meeting another across a barrier was not the greatest thing we can do for another, Buber said. The greatest thing is to confirm the deepest thing the other person has within. *The deepest thing.*[9] A friend does that by taking the time to look deeply at our soul's longings and discoveries, recognizing and encouraging that part that too often gets submerged in our frenetic times.

In an age of superficial, almost instant everything, we need these saner, more sober presences. For all the technological wonders of the modern world, you cannot characterize it as particularly deep. We dazzle ourselves with leaps in knowledge and information, but we are not known for profundity. We suffer from a glut of data but a dearth of wisdom, like the "hollow men" of T. S. Eliot's poetry. We need other influences to keep us spiritually on track. When competing voices, from glitzy ads to pressures at the office, lure us astray, we need solid people who keep us spiritually sane, spiritually alert.

JOIN YOUR ASPIRATIONS WITH THOSE OF OTHERS

Go to any "self-improvement" section in a bookstore, as I did recently, hunting for a title, and you will be overwhelmed by all the possibilities. Books on managing stress, chasing success, and affirming your inner child. We tend to think we need psychological experts to set us straight. And I have found useful information in such books. Or I have benefited from a professional counselor when I needed advice on a tough stretch of parenting. But to grow in prayer I don't need an expert as much as I need a fellow traveler. I know more than I practice. I understand more than I have the will to accomplish. I mostly need people to share the task of prayer with. Our vague spiritual aspirations waver and wither under the hot sun of secularism or skepticism or just plain spiritual laziness. "We desperately need men and women at our side," writes Eugene Peterson, "who have disciplined their minds to think *God*: who God is and what he is doing in and among us; what it means to be created and chosen by God and how we get in on what he intends for us."[10] I need someone to join a voice with my sometimes faltering praying.

Time and again, I have thrown myself into a stressful situation, griping, wringing my hands, only to have a spiritual friend say quietly, "How much time have you spent sitting in God's presence this week?" There's something about that insistent question that keeps me focused on priorities, that reminds me that the goal of life is pleasing and glorifying God, that helps me remember the resources found only in faith. Without encouragement I forget how I am to live and to pray.

Which points to the larger place of community yet again. I know that many think of going to church or other religious gatherings as "institutional religion." But in another sense to stand with others in worship is to find ourselves in the company of friends. It is to join a community of longing and trust that keeps my faith from being a freelance, private occupation. Sometimes I need more than *a* friend; I need a gathering. I need to be part of a larger movement of souls seeking and honoring God. I know that every Sunday I can find a place where others will be. Not perfect people, of course, but people looking in the same direction as I hope to. People whose praying and worshiping join forces with mine.

One way to describe my dilemma in waking up is forgetting: I forget to stay aware of God—remembering what God has done in my past, in my family's stories, in the lives of people I meet. Friends who know me help me remember. And when I go to church I align my life with others who are trying not to forget. Singing, joining in the prayers, hearing the Scripture read and preached—all help me to recall what I might lose, to see what I often miss. This motley, imperfect group becomes a spiritual community. "It is a powerful reminder simply to be in the presence of such friends," writes Gerald May. "Worship services are in part intended to help you remember what is most important in your life."[11] I need insights, modeling, sometimes just plain common sense, that I cannot muster from within myself. As Ecclesiastes put it, "Two are better than one. . . . A cord of three strands is not quickly broken." Soul friends, like Kevin, like Chris, like others I have not named—and the friends I see every time I go to worship—help me gain my footing. They help me better live the rhythms of life and prayer.

Chapter 9

THE
HARD, HIDDEN
Graces
OF SUFFERING

The heart is stretched by suffering, and enlarged.
THOMAS KELLY

Yesterday, during a twelve-hour period, on an otherwise pleasant day, I was a witness to ample suffering.

Driving to my office, I heard on the radio the story of a fifteen-
year-old who, from the time she was four, was sexually molested—
thrice weekly—by her father. Her mother looked the other way. But
the girl finally broke the awful silence by confiding in the speaker,
who was telling her story on the program.

Once at my office, a memo awaited me with news of a coworker's brother. He had learned he had lung cancer only three and
a half weeks earlier. By the time he heard the diagnosis it had spread
to the kidneys. Here it was, not even a month later, and he was
dead.

Then that evening's news told of two men nabbed in Nevada
on suspected possession of anthrax. Officials hinted about a plot to
unleash the plague germs on subway commuters. The suspicions
were soon dismissed as exaggerated, but not before the news media

frightened millions with information about just how possible such deadly prospects were.

It's not hard to get more personal about my own suffering: the six hours of desperate agony I endured from a kidney stone a couple of years ago, pain that left me nauseated and sweating. There were the years of keen self-consciousness and shyness I felt in college.

Or there was the chilling diagnosis my brother and I heard years ago.

My father had just passed away and Kevin and I began noticing that something was wrong with my mom's concentration. She couldn't remember little things or do everyday tasks. We were worried. "Transient ischemic attacks" the doctor told us—minor strokes that, with their cumulative power, could slowly unravel a life. Little did we realize that we would see my mother's condition mimic the terrible symptoms of Alzheimer's disease. Over the years, we watched her agonizingly slow decline. I once heard a husband whose wife had Alzheimer's, put it: "You don't get to say good-bye once; you say good-bye a lot of times." I would watch different pieces of Mom disappear, different parts of herself that I had known, quarreled with, loved. During one visit at her home she knew me, at least vaguely. The next time I saw her she could not, for all her pleasantness and politeness, come up with my name.

No one is unacquainted with sorrow. Because I am human and live among humans, I face painful realities and sometimes unjust miseries. I witness things that are horrible in the deepest sense of the word: they create horror. And even when cataclysms stay far from my doorstep, I deal with daily stresses that wear me down. Sometimes, during a protracted job on some manuscript I edit to pay the bills, my boredom becomes a kind of anguish in itself.

Yet many of us, when honest, find ourselves surprised when difficulty comes knocking. A part of us hopes that maybe with luck (or providence) we can escape. *Maybe I will be exempt,* I think. God will protect. Poet Donald Hall chronicled his struggle with the leukemia that took his wife's life in a collection of poems, one of which reads,

> . . . *Inside him,*
>   *some four-year-old*
> *understood that if he was good—thoughtful,*
>   *considerate, beyond*
> *reproach,* perfect—*she would not leave him.*[1]

Perhaps it is worse for modern people; we pull pills off a shelf to quiet our pain. We wave the TV remote for numbing amusement that keeps us from facing our hurts. We switch on computers to pull us from the teeth of information chaos—instantly. We get incensed when some pangs cannot be medicated, psychologized, or entertained away. Random violence, betrayal, loneliness, death, leave us feeling puzzled, even betrayed.

But unwelcome misery visits us all sometime. "I would like to make a motion that we face reality," comedian Bob Newhart was fond of saying. No matter how careful I am, no matter how faithful, I get passed over for a job promotion, I weep when someone I love rejects me, I grimace when disease haunts me. Our wisest spiritual teachers remind us that no life, no matter how charmed, forever escapes hardship. "Those who seek to avoid suffering," writes Thomas Merton, "are those who end up suffering the most. They are troubled by every little thing as well, even as they move inexorably to the suffering that is to come."[2]

Will what we believe and pray hold through the hard moments and long months? It must withstand the harrowing effects of chemotherapy, the searing pain of divorce. Can we find God in an intensive-care-ward waiting room? And there are the daily annoyances, the chronic nuisances that stoop our shoulders. How can I stay alert to God when trouble comes knocking and makes it hard to keep my mind on anything but the hurt and stress?

DON'T MAKE SUFFERING A PUZZLE TO SOLVE AS MUCH AS A MYSTERY TO FACE

Many wise thinkers have labored to make sense of suffering over the centuries. They have strained to explain the ways of God to humankind. And the explanations help, to a point. They tell us that good often comes out of evil, redeeming it; that people may emerge from hardship more conscious of what matters. "I knew that I would come out either bitter or better," someone once told me of his struggle with a painful illness. I recall, too, that Jesus said there would be a cost to following Him, a cross I would take up and bear, He said, meaning by that cross more than mild inconvenience. And we can remind ourselves that the hardship we see is often not the result of a loving Father as much as the consequences of undisciplined children who have misused their freedom and hurt others.

Sometimes the logical answers help me, a kind of solid truth to hold on to when I battle discouragement or stinging hurt. But ultimately there is much we simply cannot figure out. The questions cannot be answered too glibly. Those who suffer do not need off-the-cuff reassurances about God always bringing good out of evil. The long-suffering Job of the Bible had three "friends" who reduced

Job's misery to platitudes and pious variations on the theme that God was punishing him. I don't want my affliction brushed aside with a quick, "Suffering builds character," anymore than Job did. Or even worse, a pious, "God must be punishing you." Some suffering is too awful neatly to relegate to the dustbin of "improvement." No, "solutions" do not satisfy when every part of us cries out.

For all our attempts to explain and understand, then, suffering stands ultimately beyond concise comprehension. A spiritual outlook does not drain suffering of all its mystery. Things sometimes seem unfair. Events needlessly cruel. We still have not been made privy to all the mechanisms of the universe.

As a young teenager, Elie Wiesel was deported to a Nazi death camp, where he witnessed the hanging of an innocent boy whom Wiesel calls a "sad-eyed angel." Not long after, Wiesel recounts, he and his fellow prisoners observed the Jewish holiday of Rosh Hashanah in the camp.

"Blessed be the Name of the Eternal!" cried the voice of the officiant.

Then, writes Wiesel, "Thousands of voices repeated the benediction; thousands of men prostrated themselves like trees before a tempest.

" 'Blessed be the Name of the Eternal!'

"Why, but why," laments Wiesel, "should I bless Him? In every fiber I rebelled. Because He had had thousands of children burned in His pits? Because He kept six crematories working night and day, on Sundays and feast days? Because in His great might He had created Auschwitz, Birkenau, Buna, and so many factories of death?"[3]

What can we say sometimes, indeed? We experience moments

when, as one articulate priest of the Episcopal Church whom I know says, life strikes us mute, unable to speak.

And sometimes we should not jump to words. It is not mental gymnastics that help us hang on and grow through suffering. Textbook logic will not keep our souls awake to God. I pound on heaven's door in desperation when I must. But when no release from the pain comes, when suffering rolls on like a juggernaut, when disease, hunger, racism, fanatical oppression carry on, I let go of insisting that every question get answered. I pray not for a rationale as much as for reassurance. Not a theology lecture, but the conviction that I am loved, whatever happens.

Precisely when I acknowledge and face my vulnerability can I begin to relax. I may still hurt, but I stop expending energy trying to deny my lot. I give up, at least in part, trying to avoid the inevitable suffering that is part of all life. And I thereby open myself in a more radical way to the true hope.

When my mom slowly, piecemeal, lost consciousness from her ravaging strokes, I sometimes wondered about her soul. In no sense did she die as I normally pictured someone dying. Month after month, year after year, there was less of her, less of the woman I had known, stripped of all means of recognizing a loved one, robbed of understanding what words mean. Her speech was reduced to jabbering. I witnessed a great loss, and it was a mystery. How much of her was still "there"? The part of her soul that was gone—where did it go?

I had known her always as a woman of deep faith, telling me as I grew up how important prayer was to her. "I don't see how people get through suffering without God," she told me more than once. And I wondered, as I watched her slow slide toward oblivion, how much she was able to think about the One she had known all her waking life. Could she still sense a God who in wordless grace came close? I could not ask her, of course. If she understood the words in the first place, she certainly could not form words to answer.

But I did not despair that she was abandoned by God. I sometimes even felt I was in the presence of the holy when around her. With whatever shred of consciousness she moved through her last, almost vacant days, I choose to believe her soul lived in spiritual communion, held in the arms of a God she could not hear or explain but only feel.

And sometimes that Presence is what we know for sure. It is not everything, but enough. We may get only glimmers, but they make all the difference. They allow us to say yes to God even when we do not understand. And when we wake up to God we begin to see that we go through life with a presence of immense and comforting love.

"Is not a picture painted on a canvas by the application of one stroke of the brush at a time?" asks seventeenth-century spiritual writer Jean-Pierre de Caussade. "Similarly the cruel chisel destroys a stone with each cut. But what the stone suffers by repeated blows is no less than the shape the mason is making of it. And should a poor stone be asked, 'What is happening to you?' it might reply, 'Don't ask me. All I know is that for my part there is nothing for me to know or do, only to remain steady under the hand of my master and to love him and suffer him to work out my destiny. It is for him to know how to achieve this. I know neither what he is doing nor why.' "[4]

FIND A WAY TO LET SUFFERING
NOT DRIVE YOU FROM GOD
BUT DRAW YOU TO GOD

I once talked with a professor of spiritual theology. If you had a question about any figure in the long history of spirituality, he could spin long discourses. He was brilliant, learned. When he learned of my interest in spirituality, and some of my struggles, he told me, "I have learned that when I meet someone with a strong interest in the spiritual life, this is a person who has suffered." He knew, as someone he doubtless studied once said, the places where God communicates to us is our wounds. Catherine of Aragon, the first wife of Henry VIII, the king notorious for going through wives, went so far as to say, "None get to God but through trouble." What she suffered did not separate her from God, but propelled her to God.

God certainly has used suffering to get my attention. Does God cause devastation? Does God compel people to hurt me? No. But God uses tragedies, whatever their cause, to underline His willingness to come near. I think of an Eastern Orthodox priest who once said that he hesitated sometimes praying for healing for his parishioners because sickness was so good for their souls. That may sound callous, but I also know that once I realize I cannot control everything, that much of what happens in life is beyond predicting, I am more likely to turn to God. Perhaps it should require suffering to turn me to God. But God takes full advantage of the situation to redeem our sorrow. He wakes us up through it. "God whispers to us in our pleasures, speaks in our consciences, but shouts in our pain: it is his megaphone to rouse a deaf world."[5] Disappointment drives me to my knees. Suffering opens me up to comfort or reality that I, in my pride and self-sufficiency, might not otherwise go seeking.

Author Peggy Noonan wrote about a friend who had been very sick, and whose friends—"worldly people, well-educated, successful, and sophisticated"—kept saying, "I am praying for you, our prayers are with you." Peggy marveled that these people, many of whom in other circumstances would speak frankly of doubts about God, really did believe in the sacred. "This is my theory," she wrote. "Almost everyone knows there is a God, but some know it in an unknowing way. They don't think about it, they don't notice it, but deep down they have an unarticulated knowledge that God is real. I am still pondering it, but I think of lot of them spoke of God because they really do believe in Him, but in the past they haven't fully noticed."[6] Suffering awakened their awareness and hunger.

Some months ago I had a dream. I don't remember many details, but something happened in it that made me feel terrible. I failed someone's expectations. The feeling of plunging self-esteem was so vivid it made up for the fuzziness of the other details. I despaired. Then part of me became frustrated that events could make me so thoroughly question myself. In the dream I remember thinking, *Well, if my self-image is so vulnerable to bruising, I will use that as an occasion to turn to God. I will try to make God my sufficiency and strength.*

Once awake that morning, in my regular course of Bible reading, I came across a verse in Psalms, a prayer of King David's uttered while he was assailed by enemies, the details of which we can only guess. But what he faced drove him, as it drove me, into the only sure strength:

> *Keep me as the apple of your eye;*
> *hide me in the shadow of your wings*

from the wicked who assail me,
from my mortal enemies who surround me. (Psalm 17:18–19)

And that is what God did, and does. He hides me when danger approaches—threats to my inner and outer self, as a mother bird her young, safe in her protecting wing. "For your sake we face death all day long," Paul the apostle, no stranger to suffering wrote, echoing a psalm. "We are considered as sheep to be slaughtered."

But something kept him awake to God and unwilling to despair: "I am convinced that neither death nor life, neither angels nor demons, neither the present nor the future, nor any powers, neither height nor depth, nor anything else in all creation, will be able to separate us from the love of God that is in Christ Jesus our Lord" (Romans 8:38–39).

Rebecca Faber lives in California's Silicon Valley. Some time ago her husband came home early to clean the swimming pool; he was leaving on a business trip the next day.

Rebecca took eighteen-month-old William out of his high chair, letting him toddle around under Bob's watchful eye, while Bob continued to work on the pool.

"William's not as afraid of the water as he once was," Bob warned. But Rebecca assumed William's fear would still keep him well away. Besides, Bob had agreed reluctantly to look after him. She thought he would be fine.

Somehow, though, in the next fifteen minutes Bob worked his way down to the other side of the pool. And during that span of time little William fell into the pool. Before anyone noticed, it was too late. Soon Bob was slamming against the locked back door with William in his arms. Rebecca, frantic, dialed 911 and held the phone, waiting for a response. Finally the frantic father ran with the child in his arms to the fire station in the next block. Rebecca had the scene etched in her mind: "I saw Bob pacing under blue sky and green grass and my [lifeless] son at the back of the fire station with large men in uniform standing around him."

He never revived.

"It's an amputation," Rebecca says. The numbness began to wear off and pain became so strong that life became a "day-by-day, hour-by-hour thing to get through," recalls Rebecca. She did not always feel God's presence. "There are times it is so dark we are unaware that He's there. . . . but I found that God did come to me as I cried out to Him in a very simple way."[7] Suffering became an occasion of encounter.

But there is a complicating problem. Is not suffering sometimes God's judgment? Does it not represent God's punishing hand? I have heard people in the middle of terrible experiences seem convinced that God was bludgeoning them for some sin. And if that is the case, suffering *will* separate us from God. It will create in us the dulled resignation of a child cowed from affliction. That is what happened with Sarah, devastated by a brutal rape, who lay in her hospital bed, wringing her hands, moaning, "I must have done something really terrible for God to have punished me this way." She cringed before God.

Once her caretaker got over her astonishment that Sarah would think God had caused such horror, she began a conversation in which she tried to help Sarah consider another view. Far from God's will being the source of her hurt, she tried to say, it had been

God's will working within her that had enabled her to do and say the things that helped her survive a night of bloodying assault.[8]

To say that we *deserve* illnesses or natural catastrophes is to misunderstand. It will guarantee that we will want little of this cruel God. No, we understand religion's talk of God's wrath differently. We remember that God always, ultimately, desires good. He may allow difficult circumstances to come our way, but never as ends in themselves, always with a view to our waking up. "The language used regarding the wrath of God is to be understood figuratively," wrote the third-century theologian Origen, "for it is as if one were to call the words of a physician 'threats,' when he tells his patients, 'I will have to use the knife, and apply cauteries, if you do not obey my prescriptions, and regulate your diet and mode of life in such a way as I direct you.' "[9] God may discipline us, but it always comes as a good-hearted discipline, never meanness. God does not strike people with cancer, He does not "take" our loved ones, He does not start wars. But He warns us that certain paths lead to particular ends. "God is the only comfort," wrote C. S. Lewis. "He is also the supreme terror: the thing we need most and the thing we most want to hide from. He is our only possible ally, and we have made ourselves His enemies. Goodness is either the great safety or the great danger—depending on the way you react to it."[10]

God can redeem the worst of suffering, pain, and death. And He does. But the world is constructed in a way that to go against the grain of the order of things is to invite difficulty. Walk a ledge of a high-rise and you may fall to your death. Live a certain lifestyle or eat a certain way and you increase the likelihood of disease. Some people bring suffering on through a stubborn refusal to live as God intends. Certain sins will find us out because the universe has a moral order at its heart. Part of waking up, then, means discovering God's ways and learning to walk in them.

And whatever the source of our pain, God will use it redemptively, never destructively. God will even grieve with us, sorrowing perhaps more than we do. Sorrowing as surely He did when His own Son was strung up on a cross and left to die.

LET SUFFERING POINT YOU TO HIDDEN JOYS

"I'm learning to thank God even in the uncomfortable situations," my friend Joan once said. She had just gone through months of fatigue from a draining illness. But it was not without its learnings. There are things we see only because difficult, stressful moments make us look harder. Some insights hit a workaholic when he lies flat on his back from an illness's forced rest. Awareness of ourselves may come when someone snubs us. And we may discover just how much our friends care. We experience support we might never otherwise be privileged to see. Through much of life, we coast along until a crisis, until a long absence, until a daily stress makes us suddenly notice.

A woman I've never met but corresponded with wrote of difficulties she has being a single mother without a car. But even in those stresses have been surprising discoveries.

> The other day I was at the daycare center telling my son to get his coat on because it was raining and we didn't have a ride home that night. It wasn't that far and it wasn't raining that badly, but a woman I

thought was a stranger came up and offered a ride. It turned out that several years ago she had offered me a ride in the pouring rain. I normally wouldn't have trusted a stranger, and I wanted to refuse, but the Lord prompted me to accept, so I trusted her. It turns out that all those years—even though I had never seen her again—she and her son had been praying for me. A little while back, my son had come to this daycare center and her son and my son became friends. It was her little secret that they were both praying for us!

While most of us don't consider it a blessing to spend years without a car—especially if you're a single mom with a small child—one of the many blessings it has brought to me is an abundance of strangers who look out for me, help me in whatever way they can and pray for me. Since this has started happening, the Lord has been blessing me richly in so many different ways.

And the blessings go deeper. Says spiritual writer Simone Weil, "It is in affliction itself that the splendor of God's mercy shines, from its very depths, in the heart of its inconsolable bitterness."[11] God's mercy may be difficult to see. The outward events may leave us broken, with less bodily strength than we had, our souls bruised, our hearts tired. But we can still receive God's love, His severe mercy.

Writes one woman,

I wake in the middle of the night, and count, dollar by dollar, what we have coming in and what money has to go out. We'll make it through the month, but Johnn doesn't get another check until January 14. I may have to borrow cash from the credit cards to make the mortgage payment. Nobody knows how long the layoffs will continue. I'm trying to find a job, and it's hard to look good when I'm in a state of panic. I've bought the children Christmas presents on holiday dollars, but won't have the money to pay of the bills when they come due in February. Dear God, I am utterly afraid. How can I celebrate Christ's birth in these conditions? I need to turn over my fear. . . . I can't afford to lose faith. Johnn's awake too, though he stayed in bed while I got up to write [in my journal]. I hear him tossing. We need a sign. You have our attention, God. Please help us get our lives back in order. I remember how Grandma used to say, "When God closes a door, He opens a window." I will feel less afraid if I consider this sleeplessness a way of keeping watch.[12]

That's what we need, the grace to watch, to stay alert. We can awaken to God's presence even while we wait. If we know that we are not alone, we can give up our need always to figure things out. And be freed to expect hidden blessings.

A man was making his way across an Iowa pasture after having made a retreat at a hermitage, full of what he called the "spiritual blues." "It was a dark night of the soul," he said. "I felt great heaviness. I was trudging along, noticing how the snow had melted, how the grass was beginning to turn green where sunlight could find it. That's when I came across a cow plop from last year. It had a crusty top. Out of its middle grew a sweet, beautiful corn stalk. It was as though God was saying, 'Everything's okay! Out of the manure I grow beautiful things.' "

The God who can grow a green shoot of life amid the excrement can do a similar, deeper thing in the hard and blessed moments of our lives.

Chapter 10

FACING OUR
Fragility

In the end is my beginning.
T. S. ELIOT, "Burnt Norton"

Recently I applied for a life insurance policy. I had no idea it would be so unsettling.

Going into my appointment, I knew I would have to sort through plans and options. I expected questions about my lifestyle. But I had no inkling of how intensely my life would be scrutinized: Have you ever been treated for high blood pressure? Been diagnosed HIV positive? Been hot-air ballooning in the last six months (apparently high-risk, along with scuba diving)? Do you smoke? Then there were questions about my family history—diabetes, cancer, heart disease? And because I had just turned forty, the office assistant said the company mandated blood and urine tests. When the affable nurse came to my home to take my "samples," she had her own questions, pressing for details on my mother's cancer and my father's heart problems. By the time it was over I had answered dozens of detailed, searching questions.

I felt more than my privacy assailed, but also my sense of

durability. I was being reminded of things that could go wrong. I saw anew the fragility of life. The experience made me feel like Patrick Keane, the character in Jay McInerney's *The Last of the Savages,* who, when an associate of his law firm suddenly dies, said, "I have to admit that the whole affair has given me an acute intimation of mortality."[1]

For all the ways I rationally tried to reassure myself, to tell myself that *of course* I was insurable, I still felt relief when, a week later, my insurance company said I'd "passed." I could count myself a worthy risk. The policy soon came by mail, a kind of down payment on my eventual demise.

I never get far from experiences that remind me of the fragility of my life and the lives of those I love. None of us do. But the good news is that what seems a morbid reality actually leads me to a more wakeful life. At least it can, when I look at death aright.

RECOGNIZE THAT WE CONSTANTLY BUMP UP AGAINST OUR LIMITS

I still remember my thirtieth birthday. In a magazine article I wrote at the time I noted how "leaving my twenties was a milestone of sorts, and I looked forward to the day that marked it." But I also grew reflective as the day wore on. I wrote of an inward tug to mull over the turns and twists of my three decades. I was wistful and curious about days to come. I stood old ambitions next to current realities, asking, "How am I faring?"

A friend of mine shared his thirtieth around the same time. His office colleagues helped him "celebrate" with a wreath of dried flowers and weeds and a single black flower. A lone helium balloon, tethered to the arrangement, featured a grim, black-clad figure. Underneath the lonely figure was scrawled a caption: "OVER THE HILL."

Of course the celebration was meant as a joke, I wrote in my article. But birthdays serve as the butt of dark humor precisely because they unsettle us. They remind us of our impermanence. They haunt us with a reminder of lives we will not touch, love we will not experience, books we may not write, children we will not bear. Our bodies will grow tired, age, lose their agility, I mused. In our day's push to tan and tone, primp and prime, we like to forget that, as Paul the apostle so bluntly put it, "outwardly we are wasting away" (2 Corinthians 4:6).

That was my thirtieth birthday. My fortieth wasn't much different. I was equally pensive. Not depressed but certainly more thoughtful than usual. Now I wonder, *What will my fiftieth be like?* Birthdays, a kind of annual mile marker, leave the fleeting recognition that the trip we're on takes us to a destination from which we will not return. This year of my life is but one of a passing, limited succession. Along with birth, death is the most universal human event.

Such talk, of course, seems odd, awkward, impolite, at least in our culture. I feel uncomfortable writing it. We sometimes act as though death is such an unpleasant topic that we would do best to avoid it altogether. And our cultural practices don't exactly help us here. Where once people routinely died in their homes, the family witness to the whole event, people now die in sterile intensive care units. Where we once considered dying to be an accepted part of living, now we rely on technology to shield us. With our hygienic hospitals and stainless funeral homes we find it easy to avoid death's reminder that all is not eternal. The youthful vigor of Hollywood celebs seems instead to provide the unspoken model for a fulfilling, wakeful life. Good health becomes an almost religious pursuit, our health clubs like temples to youthful virility and power, replete with initiation rites and rituals. "Health is a dawn to dusk regimen," argues one writer, "with plenty of bedside reading. Books on health have displaced books on philosophy as sources of meditation."[2]

As one who jogs regularly and watches cholesterol in the hope of avoiding the heart disease that took my father's life, I believe in care of the body. But the thud and pant of our workouts take on a zeal with roots in something else: a determined, desperate effort to avoid our mortality. "When you've got your health, you've got everything," people say. Polled Americans list health at the top of their concerns—above love, work, money, or anything else. It seems to offer the primary source of happiness. Why? Health helps us forget the finality of our frailty. Sometimes we are like those who attended a lecture by the noted authority on care for the dying, Elizabeth Kubler-Ross. She asked the gathering, "How many here are terminally ill? Raise your hands." A few did, prompting her to say, "My dear ones, we are *all* terminally ill." And sometimes we don't just bump into the realization, we trip over it, get shaken awake by it, collide with it. Writes Frederick Buechner, "It is no longer just in my mind that I know I am rather a good deal closer to the end of my time than I am to its beginning. I know it in my stomach."[3]

Rather than depressing or dispiriting me, however, I find thinking about my limited life span is a tonic for the soul. It need not always elicit a hangdog inner moan. Not if I set my thinking in a certain context. Not if facing death leads to a more wakeful life. Death sets around me boundaries; to think about it helps me understand the limits proper to my humanity. I find myself stripped of my overblown idealisms. It tells me I cannot forever nurse godlike aspirations. No, I am a creature with limits:

Show me, O Lord, my life's end
and the number of my days;
let me know how fleeting is my life.
You have made my days a mere handbreadth;
the span of my years is as nothing before you.
Each man's life is but a breath. (Psalm 39:4–5)

Why pray to know how fleeting our days are? I uncover a bittersweet freedom in not having to be an immortal. I find a clarity. in trying, as Francis of Assisi bid his followers before his death, to "know what is mine to do." No less, no more. And in doing so I can give up the pressure to be indispensable. I can relax and be content to be a human being. Sixteenth-century church reformer Martin Luther wrote, "Even in the best of health we should have death always before our eyes [so that] we will not expect to remain on this earth forever, but will have one foot in the air, so to speak." There is a lightness to that picture, a willingness not to take our lives too seriously, which ultimately makes life richer.

When Michael Korda battled prostate cancer, he wrote,

I had come to the realization—much delayed, some would say—that I was neither immortal nor young. Cancer is a harsh teacher. It reminds us that disease and death are still out there, unappeased by vitamin-mineral supplements, low-fat diets or a perky, upbeat attitude.

Before [on the job], I had been able to push myself relentlessly. Now, I knew I would never feel the same about work. Henceforth, I would do what I could and stop. I no longer wanted to please anybody but myself, something of a sea change for a person who had been working 24 hours a day to please others for most of his adult life."[4]

Whatever its pain or poignancy, a brush with our mortality unhooks us from having to be and do everything. And facing the loss of others can likewise remind me of my limits.

Last night, drifting off to sleep, I thought with a start how few mementos I have to remind me of my parents' lives—stones tumbled smooth from my dad's jewelry hobby; an antique, chiming mantel clock; a modeling photo of my mother when she was twentysomething; my birth plate, with painted-on details of when I was born and how much I weighed. These are the things I have to keep. But most of the physical reminders of my parents' decades on this earth are gone. That awareness jolted me out of my half-asleep state, even though it has been almost two years since my mother died, and several more since a heart attack took my dad. I thought especially of the boxes of photos, mostly black-and-white, taken with my parents' ancient Brownie box camera. Only a few sit in my desk drawer, only a handful in my brother's house.

The reason was painfully simple—the dementia that my mom had shown months, even years, before my dad died accelerated once he was gone. Every time I would visit Mom from out of state, she seemed that much worse, one month unable to remember where she put her keys, six months later not always sure who I was, one year later completely unable to recognize or identify me, her youngest son. One December she was walking, able to get around. Months later she was bedfast. Those were long, poignant years.

And what happened to my mom explained why so many of the hundreds of family photos vanished. With her waning consciousness, Mom would sort endlessly through the photos, the old check registers, the kitchen recipes. She would spend her days rifling through them, creating little piles all over the house. Some photos ended up in garbage bags, put there inadvertently, I suppose, by the nurses who cared for her in her house. Most have been lost.

That remembrance symbolizes the limits of life, etched in every death, limits that I cannot live without facing, owning. Most of the time we would rather avoid the reality altogether. I miss my parents. I miss Bruce Austin, a member of my church who was killed instantly when a semitrailer truck skidded and toppled across the median divider, right onto Bruce's car. People will miss me when I am gone. I rightly hold on to some things, like life—tightly. I resist going gently into that good night, to echo the poet Dylan Thomas. But life is transitory. We tell ourselves that we are going to die, but our daily actions and thoughts reveal how hard we find it to accept.

Death terrifies, rips from us those we love, but it does not render life meaningless. While it sets before us certain painful confines, while it borders even the longest, most vigorous life, we need never forget how to live and love, in spite of death's presence, and to some extent, because of death's presence. We make peace with it, in a way, as one of the realities of what it means to live and breathe.

LET OUR COMMON FRAILTY MAKE YOU
MORE GRATEFUL, MORE AWARE

When my father died some years ago, it took two days until I finally shed tears. I had come to Santa Monica, just missing by hours being with him in his death. During those days I stayed in my old bedroom on the second floor of the house, with a view of the California coast less than a mile in the distance. As the numbness wore off, what finally prompted my grief to spill out cleanly that second day was a little thing.

The ocean breezes billowing my curtains awakened me that morning. Oddly, I found myself thinking about some textbooks I had left at home from college days. Especially two Western civilization volumes, two large reference works worth keeping. Not long before his heart attack, Dad had promised to package and mail them to my house in Texas. He hadn't gotten around to it before his heart attack and since I was home I had begun rummaging for them in my closet the day before. With a coffin and grave site and scores of other details to attend to, I gave up my search quickly. I had many more important things to do, including giving care to my mother. But still, waking up, I wondered where they had ended up.

And that's what finally did it: Lying in bed that morning, preparing to begin the day, I wanted to ask Dad where those books were. The question brought the thudding realization known to any who loses someone dear: *He is not here*. I could not ask him about *anything*. The finality of his absence broke open the bottled-up grief. I wept on my pillow, there in the room in which I had grown up, the room he had made his own study when I left home, filled with my old toys and his books and jewelry tools that made the room his own. Knowing he was no longer there to do a small kindness underlined how much I would miss my father. I felt grateful for what he had meant, for all the ways he had reached out to me and my family in the last years of his life. My tears declared an unspoken, grieving thank you for his having been a part of my life.

To lose someone, to face our own death, puts everything in sharper relief. It casts a light on how valuable, irreplaceable the intangibles are. Death has a way of making our little annoyances not so maddening. If absence doesn't always make the heart grow fonder, the prospect of the ultimate separation may make the heart grow sweeter. Death intimidates, but it also calls out to us, *Enjoy this person. Enjoy this time together. You will not always have what you have now.*

Awareness of the temporariness of my own life has a similar effect. People who have looked death in the face and lived to tell seem more settled, less ruffled. Thinking about our death makes us ask, What are the animosities in my life that should be healed, the conflicts reconciled, the favor I've put off that should be done today? "When a man knows he is going to be hanged in a fortnight, it concentrates his mind wonderfully," Samuel Johnson said. Death requires us to focus on what matters.

Like everyone, I suppose, I've had narrow scrapes, occasional times when I narrowly missed being hit by a car, only to feel a flood of relief over being spared. Almost always I breathe thanks for the chance to keep enjoying what I have, the challenges I face, the people I love, the life I lead, for all its sometimes littleness. Sometimes I pick up a phone and make that call that I had been putting off. I see life differently.

I think of the harrowing time I went flying with my friend Reynolds. He flew a two-seater plane, large enough only for two to squeeze in. We flew from a small airport north of Houston, near where I lived at the time, to Oklahoma, where we both had business meetings with a coalition of churches. It seemed a good way to cut back on the cost of airline travel and escape the long hours of a car trip.

As my wife dropped me off at the runway and I got into the beige, single-engine plane, the phrase *traveling light* took on new meaning. The storage area, just behind our seats, could hold only our briefcases and small flight bags. Anything more, Reynolds told me, and we risked overburdening the plane's modest engine.

We took off in a roar, and the view out the little window to my right was awe-inspiring. Snaking interstate highways, wooded knolls, sprawling estates, we could see it all. Nothing since has ever made me feel quite so *up there* like the thin frame of glass (or was it Plexiglas?) between me and the vast reaches below. But it wasn't just the spartan plane that made me feel precariously suspended. It was the "thermals." This was summer, and we were traveling over brown, baked Oklahoma fields, Reynolds explained. The heated earth below sent up currents of air, only to be followed by the cooler currents hovering over wooded hills. We found ourselves lurching up and down. Sometimes we would glide along, only to drop precipitously, my stomach feeling as if it were still fifty feet up, where we had been seconds before. My palms grew sweaty.

Reynolds began showing me the dials, the communications radio, the levers. We talked a bit about how you landed the thing, how a control tower could coach and guide a plane in if someone in the cockpit who has never flown before had to take over. I marveled at the sights, but prayed my way through that two-hour trip, as I did on the return leg, two days later, when our business in Oklahoma was done.

When finally I stepped out onto the tarmac at the airport near home, the sun having just set, our trip finally over, I experienced things differently. I took in the scene of Jill and the boys standing outside the just-closed terminal by our Honda wagon, waiting to take me home. The ground beneath my feet felt hard, wonderful, immovable. Professional stresses made this a tough time in my life, in many ways. But I knew after my ride how good it was to be alive. Very good.

Not many months later I learned that my friend Reynolds had to be hospitalized with a serious heart condition. He came through fine. But I thought with a sigh and a smile how I had entrusted my life to a tiny engine, to a pilot whose health could have left me soaring thousands of feet above the ground, without help. Had I known that, perhaps I would have been even more grateful when our wheels hit the runway for home.

ALLOW DEATH TO MAKE YOU MORE AWARE OF A LIFE TO COME

Considering the fragility of this life sometimes makes me ponder the everlasting dimensions of the next. My frailty points me beyond today. In a way I have not before, I think about what the ancients called heaven, and it is changing the way I live.

For some, of course, such talk seems a bit like chasing after a vague, wispy unknown. "Pie in the sky," is the old, dismissive cliché. And some make a saying of philosopher George Santayana's a life motto: "There is no cure for birth and death save to enjoy the interval." I understand the sentiment. We can spend so much time thinking about the beginning and the end that we forget to enjoy the present, right before us.

But what awaits us beyond death helps us make better sense of what we experience now. Where we are headed affects how we travel. To know that life is not a destinationless journey helps me live more completely for a final good, an ultimate goal. For if we are indeed headed toward an afterlife, a place of reckoning and accounting, a time of reward and release, the current sacrifices will seem more sensible, less impossible. Wrote Thomas à Kempis, "Write, read, sing, sigh, keep silence, pray, bear your crosses courageously; eternal life is worthy of all these, and greater combats." The choices we make will have not just immediate consequences, but eternal ones. And eternal joys.

I grew up in a church where little was ever said about hell. Not much about heaven, for that matter. I think it embarrassed the ministers sometimes, some of whom prided themselves on being thoroughly modern. But now I see the importance of the long view. If heaven exists, however we picture it, then we miss something when we suppose that this life is everything. If some kind of hell exists (and I believe it does, though I don't believe in a literal fire), then we need to be sobered. "There's no hiding place down there," says the African-American spiritual.

For the believer, however, death opens onto a new world. "Here we do not have an enduring city," wrote a New Testament writer, "but we are looking for the city to come" (Hebrews 13:14). Or as Paul the apostle put it, "So we fix our eyes not on what is seen, but on what is unseen. For what is seen is temporary, but what is unseen is eternal" (2 Corinthians 4:18). Religious faith has always argued, to some degree or another, that meaning in life is found in part *beyond* life, in a realm where injustice is recompensed, wrong righted, faith rewarded. That the centerpiece of the Christian story is the death and resurrection of Jesus has huge ramifications for eternal life. And that story has impressive implications for daily life. Indeed, we will never live fully without reference to the longer stretch of eternity, what some older versions of the Bible call everlasting life.

Writer Annie Dillard trekked to a friend's cabin on northern Puget Sound in Washington to finish a book. She had to heat the cabin with a kerosene heater and a woodstove. But she did not know how to split wood. "What I did was less like splitting wood than chipping flints." But she had a dream one night through which she realized the problem: "You aim, said the dream—of course!—at the chopping block. . . . You aim at the chopping block, not at the wood; then you split the wood, instead of chipping it. You cannot do the job cleanly unless you treat the wood as a transparent means to an end, by aiming past it."[5] The insight helped her in her struggle to write, in her efforts to do more than simply put words on a page.

What is true about writing or splitting logs also holds a truth for living: We live fully in the moment and yet also in some sense aim past life. The future stretch of eternity provides the only backdrop that makes ultimate sense of individual moments. Because death, for all its starkness and seeming darkness, can lead to something better, we let it remind us and condition us for a life to come. We prepare not only for a good dying but for an expectant leave-taking. A farewell to what is, but also an opening to what will be.

Such talk has a proper context, of course. We can too quickly move, with ourselves or with grieving loved ones, to hasty assurance that a loved one is "happy in heaven." We are not wrong to grieve death, and in compelling moments of anguished loss, even curse it. Nor do we offer ourselves or our grieving friends the thin consolation of glib assurances. "There's this 'just a shell' theory of how we ought to relate to dead bodies," writes Thomas Lynch, author of *The Undertaking*. But "to suggest in the early stages of grief that the dead body is 'just' anything rings as tinny in its attempt to minimalize as it would if we were to say it was 'just' a bad hair day when the girl went bald from her chemotherapy."[6] We treat those who grieve (and ourselves when we grieve) tenderly.

Still, every now and then we get encouraging glimpses of what is possible as we face death. We see dying transfigured into a holy moment, a kind of sacrament for the living.

My friend Darrell told me of a time when this became wonderfully real:

> My stepfather-in-law arrived very ill from out of town for my daughter's wedding. Almost immediately he was hospitalized with pneumonia. Massive congestive heart failure soon followed and he grew worse with each hour. Finally, our family had to make the difficult decision to discontinue life-support. We said our parting words before the hospital disconnected the machines. Our minister soon joined us in the hospital room. He prayed for us. And then he prayed for dying Carl. He made the sign of the cross on his forehead, then said, "Fly Christian soul, into the arms of the one who made you." Carl lived a few seconds longer. Then he was gone.

I had never been present at the moment of a soul's departure. While it was deeply sorrowful, in the context of prayer, it was one of the sweetest experiences of my life.

These foreshadowings of another realm, these rumors of a glory to come for those who know God's eternal grace, can grab our soul's attention and give us hope. Because of intimations of a life beyond, I sometimes even feel great expectancy and curiosity for what moving through death to a final life will be like.

Not long ago I talked with Kathy, whose mother had died from cancer. Her mother's lung disease combined with a gradual shutdown of vital organs and for a short time the ailing woman even had hallucinations. It was a harrowing time. Her mom finally went to a hospice to await death. But it was not a glum time for Kathy. "I sat by her bed and we had wonderful talks," she told me. "And one day I said to my mother, 'Could we have a secret, something just between us? I know it's going to sound crazy. But if you die and when you get to heaven, if it's more than you ever dreamed it would be, if you are all right and see God and Jesus, would you send me one red rose?' "

Here's what happened, in Kathy's words:

My mother said, "Yes, I'll do that." It was a special moment between us. Almost an eternal moment. I knew we had a secret.

But a week later I got to thinking about our conversations. I said, "Look, Mom, about our secret: I'll be on earth and you'll be in heaven. How are you going to get the rose to me?"

She said, "Kathy, God can do anything!"

Not long after, I really focused on the demands of her ravaging disease and quickly forgot our secret. On September 16, Mom quietly slipped away. And during the emotionally involving days leading up to the funeral the secret never crossed my mind.

But then, at the funeral home, at the wake, a strange thing happened.

I was talking to a friend. Suddenly in the back of the funeral home I caught a glimpse of an elderly gentleman with a cane, wearing a beret and camel-colored jacket. I didn't know him, and I was sure I had never seen him before. I turned and looked at him, as he knelt down at the prayer kneeler by my mother's coffin and put something on her hands.

I walked over and saw the most gorgeous velvet-red rose I had ever seen. I started laughing and crying at the same time, making a small scene. My brothers thought I was "losing it," but I told them what happened. Then I asked the man what had made him bring the rose. He said, "It's been on my mind all day. I just knew I had to get a rose for your mother." He was a distant relative; I'm not even sure if he had talked to my mother in years. But through him God sent a reminder of another realm to comfort us.

One Friday night some years ago, I stood by my bedroom window and listened to my downstairs apartment neighbor, standing in the parking lot below, bellowing threats to kill me. Our normal family noises, right above his ground-floor room, set off his rage—perhaps drunken rage. I had never experienced such fury. The threats left me shaking. I feared for my wife and young children. I mumbled a desperate prayer. When he stormed up the stairs outside our door, still yelling, the lock held. The fear subsided slowly, even after police arrived to calm him. And my family and I crept around the hallway by his door for as long as we lived there. I was reminded of my limits.

But with the benefit of distance from the immediate threat, I remember that whatever happens, however long or short I live, God can take even my frailty and mortality and fill it with the durability of eternity. And plant within me a lasting hope.

With each year I get older, of course, and more aware of my frailty. But I believe that something, really a Someone, undergirds my coming and going with permanence, however many (or few) birthdays I have left. That belief tells me that God will surround my coming and going with life, every day. Forever.

Chapter 11

Awake
TO THE FACES
AROUND US

It is only with the heart that one sees clearly.
ANTOINE DE SAINT-EXUPERY,
The Little Prince

On a spring afternoon in 1978, amid the bustle and stringent smell of a Pennsylvania hospital ward, I learned something painful and wonderful.

I was a twenty-two-year-old seminary student, making visits on my assigned floor as a student chaplain. That's when I met Emma, a feisty, wiry woman in her seventies. Lung cancer made it difficult for her to breathe, much less talk or walk. She had long since become confined to a bed. I didn't know it then, but she did not have long to live; she would cough and gasp her way to a slow death. I don't remember how I introduced myself, but our conversation got on cordially enough through all her shortness of breath.

"Could you get me a milk shake?" she suddenly asked. "You can get a couple of dollars from my wallet and run downstairs to the cafeteria. The nurses won't mind."

I didn't know what to say. *Wasn't my job to tend to spiritual needs,* I told myself, *not serve food?* I had patients to visit. Leave it to the nursing assistants to run down a milk shake. "No," I tried gently to explain. "I'm a *chaplain.*"

Emma rolled over in her bed—away from me. I knew then our fragile friendship was over. She brushed off my attempts to keep conversation going. When at last I volunteered to pray out loud with her before leaving, she would have nothing to do with my offer. Or me. All I could do was leave.

Later that day I told my chaplaincy supervisor about the encounter. I expected him to sympathize with me for being snubbed by a crank.

Was I wrong.

He would not let me feel indignant over Emma's frosty turnabout for an instant. The constant feeling of near suffocation from advanced lung disease, he pointed out, tempts even the most gracious person to become petulant.

"And why *shouldn't* a chaplain chase down a milk shake for a woman dying of cancer?" he grilled. "What kinder, more important thing *could* you have done for her?" Then, once Emma knew that my interest was genuine, he continued, the deeper words could have come. The offer to pray would have meant something.

Instead, my shallow piety and my unwillingness to get involved made my good intentions fizzle. I had much to learn.

Wise compassion still eludes me sometimes. I say hurtful things unwittingly (sometimes all too intentionally). I ignore need that is within my reach to help. But I take heart that my soul can continue to wake up to others. I meet God only to be gently turned toward the flesh and blood representatives of the human race I meet and live with daily. And from God I find a staying power that lets me do more than I could imagine on my own power.

Waking up to the faces around us means several simple things.

BEGIN BY NOTICING

Sometimes, when my mind won't let go of a task I'm working on, Jill will talk to me while I absentmindedly reply with monosyllables. Finally, she will say, "Are you *here*?" There is more to being with her than merely standing near. The physical mass of my body on the chair is only a part of it. A more subtle kind of presence counts even more. I need an availability that lets me *see* people, not just sit with them or brush past them, not just glance or nod.

Usually my problem is my immersion in myself. I fix attention on my wants and expectations. I invest much energy in wondering how I look, what I feel, what I can gain from a situation. "I realize that I can be with someone," confesses Sue Monk Kidd, "but on a deeper level I'm not available to them at all." She experiences what she calls attention deficit disorder of heart and soul. Frequently she resolves to try another way. "I decide to take up availability as a discipline, as a form of spiritual practice, like meditation, prayer, or scripture reading. What if I practice receiving each person with the whole of my heart, being fully present to them with a singularly attentive mind?"[1]

That would make a difference! Of course, I will still throw myself into projects that demand concentration. Some evenings I will read the newspaper or get engrossed in a novel. I still guard legitimate times for apartness, not drowning myself in the ocean of others' demands. Noticing others is not about inviting them to transgress all personal boundaries. But I should try to notice others regularly and well. I try to awaken to their hurts and wants. Especially when they need more than a quick nod or handshake or hurried hug. Especially when the need is great.

My friend Glenda is learning this. She has struggled in the past with depression. She has come to know very well, in her times of need, when someone is really present, really notices her. "At church or the office friends will sometimes ask me how I am. It's not the words they say that communicate their interest. It's when they put an arm around me or stop to listen that lets me know if they really care." Glenda learned something from all this. She tries consciously to face people she talks with. "In order to connect with a person, I need to see the face." I realized, talking to her, how many times I move from task to task, even converse with people, without really pausing to meet their eyes. This evening, after a long day of writing, sitting at the table with my family, I determined to look around the table, to lift my eyes from my plate and fork and read the faces of my children and wife. To take the time to notice their smiles, their frowns. Sometimes I just need to slow down long enough to let my heart see.

I recently saw an interesting book title: *How to Argue and Win Every Time* by Gerry Spence. My first reaction was, *Tell me more. No more getting intimidated and taken advantage of!* But the more I began to think about it, the more troubled I became. What happens when we face every encounter, each person, with the goal of carrying the day? We win verbal battles but lose the war to come out of ourselves for the sake of others. We keep ourselves from noticing what another feels and then showing sensitivity.

This missing of others' emotional cues can happen especially with someone who is grieving or hurting. We don't know what to say. We feel so much pressure to be profound that we end up avoiding the person. But the most important thing is to leave behind an agenda and let the other guide our expression. When a traditional Jewish family is in mourning and people come to visit the bereaved, I'm told, a visitor is not to speak or say much until the mourners speak. The idea is to let your bereaved friend or loved one let you know what is needed before you charge in. You see if they are numb, or need to laugh, or want to weep. Perhaps no words at all, just the balm of shared silence, will minister most. What you observe in the person in front of you—not some predetermined script—guides you. I find that freeing.

Rarely do people want us to dispense with advice, to come barging in with our ideas on how to "get over it," or "fix it." They want us. A simple presence. An ear to listen. A hand to grasp.

But such presence is usually costly. Sometimes I fear that another's need will overwhelm me. Once, when a friend lost his job, I would ask how his search for a new position was going. I would ask frequently. But as the weeks of no landing stretched into months, as his finances grew more desperate, I found it harder, scarier to ask. I feared I would become more involved than was convenient. It takes courage to ask, but still, I tell myself, look into the faces of people I need to care about.

Especially as we go deeper, stay around, become intimate. The cost of maintaining a presence to others threatens to scare us off. How do we *keep* noticing people, especially those we live with? When I meet someone I like, it is not hard at the beginning to show interest. Or when we first fall in love, then we may see nothing *but* our beloved. It's when we settle into the normal routines of love and family and work that our relational habits get lazy. Familiarity may not breed contempt in us but it often breeds indifference. We stop noticing. We overlook what Susan Muto calls the "spectacular singularity" of the people in our lives. "It is as if we walk through life with opaque patches over our eyes." Or through clouds that fog our vision.[2]

Waking up, taking off the patches, has to do with more than

new resolve, but with a wider, deeper respect for all those who populate my life. I treat people not as fixtures but artifacts of divine creativity. Not as interruptions but gifts.

A rabbi asked his disciples, "When do we know that light has appeared out of darkness?"

One answered, "When we can tell the difference between a dog and a lamb?"

"No," said the rabbi.

Another student answered, "When we can tell the difference between a palm tree and a fig tree?"

"No," again.

"Well, then, when do we know?"

"We know that light has appeared out of darkness when someone can look in the face of any human being and see the face of a brother or sister."

We need to see with our hearts to do that, not just with our eyes. We see *persons,* not objects. And we remember where people come from, and where they go. That we are not dealing with a body or function. We witness the human person—anyone we meet—as an embodiment of love and grandeur. "There are no *ordinary* people," writes C. S. Lewis. "You have never talked to a mere mortal. Nations, cultures, arts, civilizations—these are mortal, and their life is to ours as the life of a gnat. But it is immortals whom we joke with, work with, marry, snub, and exploit—immortal horrors or everlasting splendors."[3]

That view helps us relate differently. It nudges us to show a little more patience to the needy coworker who asks of us more than we want to give. We begin to see the homeless, the weak, the small, all those we might once have dismissed as unworthy of our attention, as valuable in their own right. We show respect to the people who wait our tables, who populate our office. Who share our homes.

Jesus certainly took that view. He saw *through* to the person within, created in the image of God. Even the crusty exterior of thieves and whores and government compromisers could not keep Him from seeing the needy, hungry heart within. And when, in a great vision of the end of time He spoke of an eternal reckoning for the righteous and unrighteous, the acid test had to do with treatment of the needy, the sick, the prisoner. " 'Lord, when did we see you hungry and feed you, or thirsty and give you something to drink?' " ask the righteous. " 'When did we see you a stranger and invite you in, or needing clothes and clothe you? When did we see you sick or in prison and go to visit you?'

"The King will reply, 'I tell you the truth, whatever you did for one of the least of these brothers of mine, you did for me' " (Matthew 25:38–40).

In a scene from the movie *Ironweed,* the characters played by Jack Nicholson and Meryl Streep stumble across an old Eskimo woman lying in the snow, probably drunk. Intoxicated themselves, the two debate what they should do about her.

"Is she a drunk or a bum?" asks Nicholson.

"Just a bum. Been one all of her life."

"And before that?"

"She was a whore in Alaska."

"She hasn't been a whore all her life. Before that?"

"I dunno. Just a little kid, I guess."

"Well, a little kid's something. It's not a bum and it's not a whore. It's something. Let's take her in."[4]

To notice is to see something precious in the poor, the unlovable, the outcast. "To love a person," said Russian novelist Fyodor

Dostoevsky, "means to see him as God intended him to be."[5] It recognizes a child—a child of *God*—not a "bum."

DON'T DISCOUNT THE
SMALL ACT OF KINDNESS

While waiting at a department store display counter one fall, I overheard the man next to me telling the clerk he was looking for a gold necklace. "I want something simple, but nice," he said. Just then a group of the man's friends recognized him and hailed him from across the store. As they came up, they realized what he was doing—buying a gift for his wife. "A birthday present? Early Christmas present?" they asked, laughing. "No," he said a little sheepishly, "I just wanted to get her something. . . ." Other sounds in the store drowned out their conversation, but I knew what he was saying. "I just wanted to get her something"—reaching out for a small, tangible expression of love. But no less significant for its littleness.

Some of the kindest things we do come about through the simplest, most ordinary gestures. The imagined smallness of our deed should never hold us back. The little things, whether done for a loved one or for some global cause, have great integrity. We need not sway stadium crowds to offer a kind word to a friend. We need not travel to faraway missionary territories to tell someone of God's kind love. And because we cannot slow the juggernaut of world famine does not mean we cannot share food or money to help one family. Only some feel a call to social activism, but anyone can show a kindness to someone who is homeless. Not everyone has a degree in counseling, but anyone can offer a listening ear. And we will find how attending to the little details spells out more than grand words.

"God is in the details," a famous architect was once quoted as saying. The point was that lots of people can draw up schemes for towering skyscrapers or impressive monuments. But it takes more than grand plans. At some point you have to put bolts in place, figure the stress on a girder, and design something that fits into the surrounding landscape and terrain.[6] The little things confirm the larger truths. Faith finds hands and feet.

A letter recently told me of a man named Constantino. For years, an oppressive government held him in a tiny cell. His only human contact was with his torturers. But then, through the auspices of a human rights group called Amnesty International, someone did a small thing with great ramifications. He wrote,

> I did not experience a human face or see a green leaf, and my only company was cockroaches and mice. The only daylight that entered my cell was through a small opening at the top of one wall. For eight months I had my hands and feet tied. On Christmas Eve the door to my cell opened and the guard tossed in a crumpled piece of paper. I moved as best as I could to pick it up. It said simply, "Constantino, do not be discouraged; we know you are alive." It was signed "Monica" and had the Amnesty International candle on it.
>
> Those words saved my life and my sanity. Eight months later I was set free.[7]

Sometimes the little things we do matter more than we realize. The letter, the phone call, the firewood we cut and stack, the bread we bake and bring. Even the hug we give a child. I heard of one couple who noticed that whenever the dad changed their baby's diapers, the baby cried more. The dad, a researcher by trade, wanted to find out why. He used run charts, flow charts, histograms, and other arcane tools. What they showed him was that when his wife changed the diaper, she used more eye contact. She caught the child's attention more. Dad started doing the same. And the baby cried less, reassured by the more constant sight of her father's face. Little gestures made all the difference.

"All day long we are doing eternally important things without knowing it," writes Eugene Peterson. "All through the day we inadvertently speak words that enter people's lives and change them in minor or major ways, and we never know it."[8] Sometimes we find out, and it is a grace and encouragement. Like the time I visited a friend, seriously ill with heart complications, in a hospital. "I'm so glad you came," she said. "I'm glad to see your face. I'll remember seeing you today and that will help me keep in touch with reality." We may be lucky enough, sometime, to get a glimpse of how our lives matter, like banker George Bailey in the film *It's a Wonderful Life*. Discouraged, penniless, ready to kill himself, an angel takes George on a surreal tour of what Bedford Falls would have been like without his little life. He is left speechless and reclaims his life. In the concluding scene, someone hails him as "the richest man in Bedford Falls." It always moves me, every time I see it, sometimes to tears.

We can count on the fact that the world is built on tiny acts, not grand sweeps—*our* tiny acts. My religious faith becomes visible on neighborhood doorsteps, hospital wards, refugee camps, and prison compounds. In a world where the little carries great significance, a two-dollar milk shake will shout the presence of God, as I discovered in a Pennsylvania hospital ward. And that makes all the difference—in us and in our world. That realization helps me wake up to others.

OPEN YOUR LIFE TO OTHERS
AND OPEN YOURSELF TO GOD

One March day some years ago, while I was praying, I felt God bring to my mind the name of a Ugandan refugee living in downtown Houston, not far from where I lived at the time. A mutual friend had given Byabakama my name, and I had got to know him over the course of months. He once served me a spicy African lunch at his apartment and I spent time helping him adjust to life in America. Now as I prayed and found his name coming up, I suddenly felt urged to send money. I mentioned it to Jill over lunch that day. Before I had had a chance to act on God's nudge, Byabakama called, that very afternoon, telling me of taxes and a rent payment due. I don't remember how much I gave, or exactly how I advertised his needs to people at our church, but prayer that day did more than settle me in religious comfort. It tugged on my sleeve, it opened me up. It helped wake up my conscience. I was more alert when need appeared.

I've known this to happen time and again. Someone was debating whether to call a friend undergoing chemotherapy. He turned his internal debate into a gentle prayer. "Suddenly the confusion was gone. I found myself at a place of clarity. I picked up the phone and made the call my friend desperately needed." Perhaps you have been sitting in a pew or taking a hike in the woods. Suddenly you feel a quiet compulsion, as though an imperative comes from beyond. You feel a gentle pressure. Your soul guides your hands.

The one who awakens to God awakens also to the needs of others. Prayer seldom concludes without some sense of our next step, some intimation of help to give, some heightened sense of the world around us. Once I talked with Marie LaBreque, a retired correctional officer living in a New England coastal town. When she worked at the jail, she had seventeen miles to travel to work. "As I drove," she told me, "I asked God for help for the day to come." She sought resources beyond her own. "Once I was there, if there was an inmate needing help, I would try to understand, try to say the right thing to help him out."[9] Prayer was not disconnected from her compassion, it was its source.

Sometimes we get the idea that prayer can be an escape from a world of need. Some use religion as an excuse for evading difficult situations. A character in Fyodor Dostoevsky's *Brothers Karamazov* visits a monastery and cynically concludes: "Here in the hermitage are altogether twenty-five saints saving their souls, looking at each other and eating cabbage." Sometimes I fear that times I spend praying should go to something practical, something tangible. Volunteering to help the homeless, say. Or getting up and helping my wife fold the family's laundry. And sometimes I should. Sometimes I do. But that doesn't mean always.

It is just not true that prayer leads to passive resignation, that people who pray long and deeply are of no earthly good. We may get away to gain perspective or let God refresh our tired spirits, but we do it not just for ourselves, but also for the sake of others. In prayer we gain the resiliency and power we need to keep going when helping becomes hard. "Be strong in the Lord and in His mighty power," the New Testament cautions us. "Our struggle is not against flesh and blood" (Ephesians 6:10, 12). So we face off against suffering and injustice not only with indignation but also with prayer. In the presence of God we realize it is not always true that if we all just try a little harder and "reach out and touch someone" that everything will right itself. Evil is more slippery, seductive, and pervasive than that. Abuse and injustice should make our blood simmer. Like the prophet Habakkuk, we may even raise our voices with an exasperated, "How long, O Lord?" But in God's presence our urgency becomes more than anger; it becomes holy ire that energizes. Folding our hands in prayer, one theologian remarked, can be "the beginning of an uprising against the disorder of the world."[10]

Not only is faith not an escape from responsibility then, it is the only reliable way to it. It provides precisely what we need to do what we should. Sue Monk Kidd tells the story of a summer when she was twelve:

> I had gone to a nursing home with a youth group
> from my church. Frankly, I was there under duress.
> My mother had not heard my pleas that I be spared
> the unjust sentence of visiting a nursing home when
> my friends were enjoying the last day of summer
> vacation at the city swimming pool. Smarting from the
> inequity, I stood before this ancient-looking woman,
> holding a bouquet of crepe paper flowers. Everything
> about her saddened me—the worn-down face, the
> lopsided grin, the tendrils of gray hair protruding from
> a crocheted lavender cap. I thrust the bouquet at her.
> She looked at me, a look that pierced me to the

marrow of my twelve-year-old bones. Then she spoke
the words I haven't forgotten for nearly thirty years.
"You didn't want to come, did you, child?"

The words stunned me. They were too painful, too
powerful, too naked in their honesty. "Oh yes, I
wanted to come," I protested.

A smile lifted on one side of her mouth. "It's okay,"
she said. "You can't force the heart."

I tried to forget her. For a while I hated her for the
rebuke. Then I passed it off as the twittering of an old
woman. Years later, though, as I began to follow the
labyrinth of my spiritual journey, I discovered again
the truth in her words.

You can't force the heart. Genuine compassion cannot
be imposed from without.[11]

No, Kidd realized, you don't make up your mind to be com-
passionate as much as set out on a journey with God that eventually
transforms all your life, including your affections. Love grows from
within, as a process, as a cooperative work of God's Holy Spirit. So
we turn to God and ask His help in doing what we would never do
on our own. And God will open our eyes to those around us. It will
be sheer grace that we go on. Pure gift.

STAY OPEN TO WHAT
THOSE WE HELP CAN TEACH US

How often have I "helped" someone only to realize that I was the
recipient of grace. I cannot count the times I have visited someone

in the hospital, someone grieving a loss, only to find my own faith refreshed. My own heart warmed.

I once heard about a woman, steeped in loneliness. One of her children had gone far away to college. One day she decided to volunteer in a home for mentally disturbed children. As she began visiting the children, here's what happened:

> Becoming attached to one little boy, I asked to spend some time with him. The supervisor granted permission. "But," she warned, "you've selected a difficult case."
>
> Undaunted, I tried to interest the child in games. I tried reading stories. Some days we just walked around the grounds, his hand in mine. Several times I felt his little fingers returning my grasp, but then the hand would go limp again and I would sink deeper into disappointment. I decided to tell the supervisor that my time would be spent better elsewhere. . . . That was a dreary winter day. Dejected, I was bundling up to leave when I felt a little tug at my coat. I looked down. In little eyes where for so long I had seen nothing, I saw a shining light. "Read story agin," my little boy whispered haltingly. *He had talked!* With trembling hands I gathered the child into my lap. As I finished the short book once more, my little boy snuggled closer, and for the first time fell asleep in my arms. . . .
>
> Later, while driving home I realized that I had had an experience in genuine reciprocity. Because it had been a turning point for me too. The bereft feeling

that had led me to my job was gone. I had seen for
myself that just as love begets love, need fulfills need.
It was simple, but a little miraculous.[12]

We start out thinking we are the experts, the helpers, the
caregivers. Then we discover that we also need help. The "little"
people we think about with condescension enter our lives as agents
of a vast God. We set out as savior, and find ourselves the ones
saved, brought back to our truer selves.

Chapter 12

BY FITS AND

Starts

The thoughts with which I meditated about you were like the efforts of those who would like to get up but are overcome by deep sleep and sink back again.
AUGUSTINE

No one can doubt that numberless opportunities abound, by which through God's grace the coldness and sleepiness of our minds can be shaken off.
JOHN CASSIAN

In the back of my mind, as I have written this book, I have taken its title two ways: An imperative, a declaration to my soul: "Wake up!" After all, there is effort to make, oars I need to pull, practices of soul I need to cultivate. I tell my deepest self to shake off drowsiness.

But there's another way to read the title, a reading that acknowledges I can't do this myself, that I can wake up only through grace, a reading that makes it a prayer: Awake my soul, O Lord.

I can never assume I don't need to pray it. While spiritual-ity comes naturally, it does not always progress easily. To wake up fully, I need all the resolve I can muster and all the help I can get.

As I sat in church one February morning, the pastor read a story about Jesus going up to a mountain to pray. " 'And as [Jesus] was praying,' " I heard, " 'the appearance of His face changed, and His clothes became as bright as a flash of lightning.' "

Talk about an extraordinary story! But astonishingly, I was oblivious. Here I was, sixteen rows from the front, sitting in an oak pew while stained glass shed vivid colors on the vaulted walls, and my mind was elsewhere. I had no idea what was being read. Had you sat next to me, you would have said I was there, eyes open, plaid shirt buttoned, hair in place after a morning shower. But in a real sense I was somewhere else.

Not until the pastor began his sermon, mentioning the story again, did I realize I had missed hearing the reading. Reading it again, this time paying attention, I found a double irony. Peter and the other followers who came with Jesus to His "transfiguration" on the mountain "grew very sleepy." A scene of splendor and light opened before them and they were yawning. Only when they be-came "fully awake," the story tells us, did they see the glory of Jesus.

I see myself in that story, in the bleary half-wakefulness of those early followers of Jesus. I find my experiences of waking up real, even life changing sometimes, but also sporadic. I fall back sometimes. I open my eyes only partly. I have to keep at it. To keep me at it, my soul moves me to pray in three ways:

PRAY WITH LONGING

Today has felt a bit scattered—holding the ladder for Abram while he paints the eaves and trim of the house, taking Bekah to her gymnastics class, fitting in time to write, arranging to meet my agent later this afternoon to pick up some papers. There have certainly been moments of pleasure: I am proud of Abram, who has worked hard this year to earn money for next year's college. I have watched Micah play delightedly with his sister, amazingly patient for a four-teen-year-old. Jill is off at work, appreciated by those she works with. I feel grateful as I tap away at my computer keys.

But underneath is a current of longing. You might not know it to look at me, but there is a part of me that never seems satisfied, always wants more—more of life, of security, of God. Through such moments I never seem to stop yearning for soul satisfaction.

And I think that is good.

Once when I was a pastor, I mentioned to a member of my church that I felt restless for a more vivid experience of God's presence. I saw it as reaching out for more. But Tom, a middle-aged farmer who liked his religion cut and dried, shifted uncomfortably in his seat. He was afraid I was having a crisis.

Longing, however, seems to be part of who we are. Ignored, it gnaws at us. But attended to, listened to, it changes us. One Sufi spiritual teacher, when asked how to grow in prayer, said, "Don't pray for water, pray for thirst." Surely we pray for water, too, but sometimes hunger and thirst motivate us more than complacent satiation. After all, when we see something truly beautiful, we are never satisfied with just a glimpse or pale copies. When we taste God's sweetness, our spiritual hunger leaves us unwilling to settle for cardboard substitutes. "Late have I loved you, beauty so old and new," wrote fourth-century African theologian Augustine, drawing on every sense. "You called and cried out aloud and shattered my deafness. You were radiant and resplendent, you put to flight my blindness. You were fragrant, and I drew in my breath and now I pant after you. I tasted you, and I feel but hunger and thirst for you. You touched me, and I am set on fire to attain the peace which is yours."[1]

So we do not completely come to rest. "The word *longing*," Frederick Buechner tells us, "comes from the same root as the word *long* in the sense of length . . . and also the word *belong*, so that in its full richness *to long* suggests to yearn for a long time for something that is a long way off and something that we feel we belong to and that belongs to us."[2] That says much about our soul's life with God. God is both here, and beyond. We find peace, but also an urge for more. So we begin, and begin again. We try, make headway, and sometimes fail. We forget why we were made and who made us. We fall asleep while glory passes by. We neglect the faces around us in favor of admiring our image in the mirror, or in the mirror of the approval of people around us. But then something calls us back. And our longing increases. Our soul's desire for the beauty of God, Gregory of Nyssa wrote centuries ago, is intensified by our very progress toward it. "And this is the real meaning of seeing God: never to have this desire satisfied. But fixing our eyes on those things which help us to see, we must ever keep alive in us the desire to see more and more."

Years ago, at a time of great transition and uncertainty, I stayed up late one night. It was turning winter and I sat by the window of our upstairs bedroom. I wrote in my journal, "I just heard geese outside, honking, making haunting, lofty calls, as they make their way southward through a moonlit night. I thought, *I am like them. I* am traveling, migrating, toward God and some future that I don't fully see. I barely glimpse it." While what I jotted down applied to the externals of my life, it also captured what happens—much of the time—on the inside.

PRAY WHILE WAITING

Some days I want all my ambitions fulfilled—now. Our culture has accustomed me to instancy. Microwave ovens cook food in minutes that two decades ago took hours. We even have restaurants known for "fast food." When a flight is delayed after all are on board, when I have to wait in a checkout line behind six others, I get antsy. A decade ago I would have waited days for a letter to be sent or to arrive. Now I get impatient when my e-mail memos take a couple of minutes to go through. "We live," writes Sue Monk Kidd, "in an age of acceleration, in an era so seduced by the instantaneous that we're in grave danger of losing our ability to wait."[3] We are addicted to quickness.

But in some things, like growing the soul's wakefulness, waiting is the most fruitful attitude. It cannot be otherwise. "We do not obtain the most precious gifts by going in search of them but by waiting for them," writes Simone Weil.[4] A friend of mine thinks Weil exaggerated a bit, that sentiments like that can lead to passivity. But I know what Weil means. The soul shakes out of hibernation not so much from fierce concentration as simple openness. Not gritting teeth and coercing eyelids open. No, patience and standing in readiness form our method when it comes to the divine. Some years ago I penned in my journal, during a fretful time, "This week I have been depressed with waiting doubt, with a sense of the slowness of God's purposes as we try to find a buyer for our house, find new jobs where we want to move, and take our leave from this place." I'm not now in the crisis I was then. But I also know I still fret. I live far below my soul's potential. If I could, I would live with a more steady awareness of God's presence. I would like to be unruffled whenever a publisher rejects a proposal for a book I want to write, knowing that God always works out His purposes some-how, somewhere. I hate the way I sometimes treat people as objects who can benefit me, as means to my own scheming ends. I would love people more deeply if my fallen nature did not intervene. But along with all my efforts and struggles I have no choice but to cultivate a waiting soul.

I remember once seeing a homeless woman in California stand alongside her beat-up Ford Pinto parked at a curb overlooking the Pacific Ocean, her possessions crammed onto the seats and every dashboard cranny. She stood and stared off into the blue horizon. Everything in her seemed to be waiting. Waiting, perhaps, for a break in her fortune, or perhaps for the return of someone who left and threw her life in disarray. We can all supply our own stories when waiting was difficult. And we usually see waiting as an incon-venience or even heartache. Second only to suffering, someone has said, waiting may be the greatest teacher. Or the harshest. Waiting is sometimes the most courageous thing we do. A woman I know wrote a book titled *Graceful Waiting,* dealing with her struggles to be patient with God when terrible things happened. "My waiting was anything but graceful," she told me. "The grace was on God's part."

Waiting asks us to do some necessary letting go of things we think we might want to hold on to. To wait means to stop trying always to precisely steer our little boat. Even when we do it halt-ingly, badly, trying again and again to put our hand back on the rudder. Waiting points us to a Presence who may not work out His plans on our timetable. It has us approaching life with open, even empty hands, not clenched fists. It majors on vigilant trust for what will be, not taking charge.

Much of our waiting is, of course, filled with our preferences. We have an idea of how we want things to work out: this job, that neighborhood. We'd like one relationship to end in romance, another needy person to go away and stop bothering us. "I wish" is the constant phrase of our waiting. But the waiting I have in mind is open-ended. It implies releasing power we think we want to wield. "Whenever you pray," writes Henri Nouwen, "you profess that you are not God and that you wouldn't want to be, that you haven't reached your goal yet, and that you never will reach it in this life, that you must constantly stretch out your hands and wait again for the gift which gives new life."[5] Waiting requires us to relinquish our tendency to tell God what to do.

But waiting is also a way to make ourselves ready for something more, something better, something we cannot do without. If waiting asks us to let go of what we own and where we think we want to go, it is to make room for resources beyond our own. Waiting even comes as a kind of relief because we finally can live without feeling as if everything depends on us. Self-sufficiency has never been a particularly comforting, or spiritual, ideal. But waiting is a hopeful relinquishment.

If waiting leads us to let go, it also readies us for possibilities we could not manufacture on our own. I can tell myself that even on days when nothing seems to happen, someone is at work. I may not see the tangible expression, but the reality of that divine influence and action is not less real, not less full of potentiality. And one day, as I go along in faithfulness, I might be met in the most mundane circumstance. I catch the luminescence of a rainy Saturday. Even amid tragedy I uncover splashes of joy, moments of possibility, glimpses of love from those I love.

While I am surely not talking technique, while I mean not a science but an attitude, waiting indicates an unlatching of the doors of our soul that we sometimes shut tight to life's larger dimensions. It means daily, practical, continual turns of mind and heart. We turn away from the worries that consume, the urgencies that obsess, to the opportunities at hand. So waiting, seen in this way, also creates a chance to pause and notice people around us. Bob Morris, a teacher and minister, was standing in line at the local bakery behind a "tangibly impatient woman":

> A dozen customers are ahead of us, and fewer
> salesclerks than usual. She sighs; she huffs; she shifts
> restlessly from one foot to another, checking the time.
> Her frustration agitates the air around her, rubbing
> against others. . . . She may have a right to be
> impatient, for all I know. No doubt this is not the way
> she planned to spend her time. . . . My own
> annoyance takes a deep second breath. As my right
> hand turns palm up in an unobtrusive gesture of
> prayer, the sights and sounds of this friendly bakery
> become clearer. Two young children play happily in
> the nearby kiddy corner. Sunlight streams through the
> window behind me, warming my back. It's a
> wonderful place to be on a busy Saturday morning,
> full of wholesome goodness. My favorite Hebrew
> chant, *Hineni ("Here am I")* arises in the back of my
> throat. The gift of standing here is simple, good, and

sweet. I share that goodness with the unhappy woman, surrounding her with God's light in my heart. I can't say this makes much difference in her visible behavior, but it's better than my impatience rubbing against her impatience. She treats the salesclerk with snippy sarcasm, which I, at least, am able to soothe when my turn comes next. The saleswoman smiles.[6]

PRAY AND HOPE

Not far from my house, a subdivision is being carved out of undeveloped Tennessee countryside. For months workers warred against a wilderness of hackberry trees and mammoth slabs of underground rock—chain-saw wielding woodsmen felling massive trees, diggers and tractor operators chiseling out a network of pipes and drainage channels. It took months of backbreaking labor before the first frame of a house appeared. Over the months, I have sometimes gone walking there after the workmen go home. Some of the rugged paths I first traversed are now paved roads. Swing sets adorn the backyards of prim brick homes, people clobber their morning bedroom alarms, groggily shower, and drive to work, returning to softly lit kitchens and dining rooms at nightfall. What was once only a wild woodland now is a subdivision. McFarlin Woods thrives, tamed out of a tangle of primitive, rugged nature.

In our lives, we give what we can, chip away at a more consciously spiritual life, hack our way through wilderness thickets. But we do not need to give up. For every now and then, sometimes when we least expect it, our digging and hoping yield pay dirt. We experience the Presence. And so we keep going, fortified.

That God is the one who sparked our searching for Him in the first place is good news indeed. *God* made us restless, Augustine said, until we find our rest in Him. Which means our search has an object. There's an old saying, "I chased her and chased her until she finally caught me." God repeatedly, patiently, takes the initiative. We come because He is the Great Inviter. Our finding is more a being found.

That God started all this searching of mine gives my praying great hope. "I know the plans I have for you," the Lord said through Jeremiah, the Hebrew prophet, "plans to prosper you and not to harm you, plans to give you hope and a future" (Jeremiah 29:11–13). God, whom we may sometimes fear or paint as distant or aloof, turns out to be *good*. Worthy of trust. Standing ready.

I once visited the novelist and essayist Frederick Buechner in his Vermont home. As we sat in his study, surrounded by his memorabilia—a bound volume of letters from a cherished relative, family photos, an old clock, a beer stein—he told me the story of an old, battered license plate that once hung on the wall. A "holy relic," he called it. For in a bleak time in his life he was parked by a road not far from his Vermont home, worrying about his then-anorexic teenage daughter. Suddenly, out of nowhere, it seemed, a car came down the highway with a license plate bearing the letters *T-R-U-S-T*. "Of all the entries in the lexicon of words that I needed most to hear, it was that word *trust*," he said. "It was a chance thing, but also a moment of epiphany—revelation—telling me, 'Trust your children, trust yourself, trust God, trust life; just *trust*.' "

Weeks later, Buechner was sitting in his living room with his youngest daughter talking over the very same anxieties, when, he said, "So help me, there came a knock at the door and my daughter answered it. I heard her speaking to someone and then there was a male voice that I didn't recognize. It was the owner of the license plate—the trust officer in the local bank, whose reason for the choice of the word became obvious—and he said, 'Here, I wanted you to have this.' " The man had heard Buechner tell the story in a sermon and he wanted him to have the emblem of what let Buechner—lets us all—carry on.[7]

Trust. That is why we pray in hope. That is how we pray at all. God's eyes never stray from our circumstances. Like any good parent, God patiently, lovingly provides a way from wherever we are back to His house. If we are off course or going backward or getting stuck, God will plot a way. There is always a way. Even in the dull flat stretches or on the bouldered roads, we can hope. God can break into our doldrums and make us aware, awake.

This morning I woke up to a wet, late-winter morning. There was snow mixed in with the drizzle—in Tennessee—of all things. I was tired from yesterday's work, but I put on sweats and a down vest and went running outside in the dampness anyway. And then I came across a splash of vivid, stubborn color: A neighbor had planted crocuses around his mailbox. I lingered over the flowers' cool white, warm yellow, and vibrant violet. Their petals stayed clamped shut from the lack of sun, but their colors seemed all the more vivid against the brown mulch. I stopped to look, finally fully awake, for it was as though something was saying, "There is always the promise of spring." As though God was saying, "Always the promise of spring."

AFTERWORD

I am interested in hearing about ways this book helped you in becoming aware of God in daily life. And I am interested in hearing about how you pray and what you are discovering about God. Please write to me at P.O. Box 968, Nolensville, TN 37135.

END NOTES

INTRODUCTION

1. Bernd Heinrich, *A Year in the Maine Woods* (Reading, Mass.: Addison-Wesley, 1997), ix.

2. Robert Benson, *Between the Dreaming and the Coming True* (San Francisco: Harper San Francisco, 1996), 8.

3. Avery Brooke, *Finding God in the World* (New York: Harper & Row, 1989), 1.

4. Thomas Kelly, *The Sanctuary of the Soul* (Upper Room Spiritual Classics, Series 2) (Nashville: Upper Room, 1997), 25.

Chapter 1

YOU DON'T HAVE TO BE A SAINT

1. Dallas Willard, *The Divine Conspiracy* (San Francisco: Harper San Francisco, 1998), 61.

2. Saint John of the Cross, *The Living Flame of Love,* 4:4, in *The Collected Works of Saint John of the Cross,* trans. Kieran Kavanaugh, O.C.D. and Otilio Rodriguez, O.C.D. (Washington, D.C.: ICS Publications, 1991), 709.

3. Anthony DeMello, *Sadhana* (St. Louis: The Institute of Jesuit Sources, 1979), 25.

4. C. S. Lewis, *Mere Christianity* (New York: Collier/Macmillan, 1943, 1945, 1952), 54.

5. Christopher de Vinck, *The Power of the Powerless* (Grand Rapids, Mich.: Zondervan, 1988, 1995), 55.

6. Stephen Bryant, "An Unexpected Turn," *The Upper Room,* May/June, 2.

7. Evelyn Underhill, *The Spiritual Life* (Ridgefield, Conn.: Morehouse, 1937, 1938, 1955), 24.

8. As told in Eugene Peterson, *The Wisdom of Each Other* (Grand Rapids, Mich.: Zondervan, 1998), 38.

9. Robert C. Morris, "The Second Breath," *Weavings,* March/April 1998, 37.

10. Gerard W. Hughes, *God of Surprises* (London: Darton, Longman and Todd, 1985), 5.

11. Howard R. Macy, *Rhythms of the Inner Life* (Newberg, Ore.: Barclay, 1988, 1992), 26–27.

12. Gerald May, *The Awakened Heart* (San Francisco: Harper San Francisco, 1991), 71.

Chapter 2

GOD WITHIN REACH

1. Thomas Merton, *No Man Is an Island* (New York: Harcourt Brace and Jovanovich, 1955), xiii.

2. Annie Dillard, *Pilgrim at Tinker Creek* (New York: Harper & Row, 1974), 9.

3. Augustine, *Confessions,* trans. Henry Chadwick (Oxford: England: Oxford University Press, 1991), 6.

4. Frederick Buechner, *A Room Called Remember* (San Francisco: Harper & Row, 1984), 61.

5. William Shakespeare, *Romeo and Juliet,* Act 2, Scene 2.

6. Meister Eckhart, *The Best of Meister Eckhart,* ed. Hacyon Backhouse (New York: Crossroad, 1996), 34.

7. Thomas Merton, *The Sign of Jonas,* (San Diego, Calif.: Harvest/Harcourt Brace, 1953, 1981), 102–3.

8. *The Book of Common Prayer* (New York: The Church Hymnal Society, 1979), 287.

9. Meister Eckhart, *Sermons.*

Chapter 3

WAYS WE WAKE

1. Gerald May, *Simply Sane* (New York: Crossroad, 1977), 44–45.

2. Annie Dillard, *An American Childhood* (New York: Harper & Row, 1987), 11.

3. C. S. Lewis, *Mere Christianity* (New York: Collier/Macmillan, 1943, 1945, 1952), 169.

4. Christopher de Vinck, *The Book of Moonlight* (Grand Rapids, Mich.: Zondervan, 1998), 31.

5. Evelyn Underhill, *The Spiritual Life* (Ridgefield, Conn.: Morehouse, 1937, 1938, 1955), 17.

6. Frederick Buechner, *The Sacred Journey* (San Francisco: Harper & Row, 1982), 4–5.

7. Gregory the Great, *Moralia in Iob,* Book 1, Chapter 4.

8. Annie Dillard, quoted in Robert Benson, *Between the Dreaming and the Coming True* (San Francisco: Harper San Francisco, 1996), 75.

9. As suggested by Douglas Steere, *Dimensions of Prayer* (Nashville, Upper Room Books, 1997), 13.

10. Henri Nouwen, *Making All Things New* (San Francisco: Harper & Row, 1981), 23–24.

11. Jean-Pierre de Caussade, quoted in Gerald May, *The Awakened Heart* (San Francisco: Harper San Francisco, 1991), 73.

12. Jean-Pierre de Caussade, *The Sacrament of the Present Moment,* trans. Kitty Muggeridge (New York: Harper & Row, 1981).

13. Truman Capote, *A Christmas Memory* (New York: Random House, 1956), 42–43.

14. Maurice Grosser, *The Painter's Eye,* quoted in Betty Edwards, *Drawing on the Right Side of the Brain,* 4.

15. Kathleen Norris, *Cloister Walk* (New York: Riverhead Books, 1996), 1.

16. Thornton Wilder, *Our Town,* in *Three Plays by Thornton Wilder* (New York: Bantam, 1957), 61–62.

Chapter 4

EYES AND EARS OPEN

1. Esther de Waal, *Living with Contradiction* (San Francisco: Harper & Row, 1989), 79–80.

2. C. S. Lewis, *Letters to Malcolm, Chiefly on Prayer* (New York: Harcourt Brace Jovanovich, 1963), 90.

3. Evelyn Underhill, *The Spiritual Life* (Ridgefield, Conn.: Morehouse, 1937, 1938, 1955), 22.

4. C. S. Lewis, *Letters to Malcolm, Chiefly on Prayer* (New York: Harcourt Brace Jovanovich, 1963), 90.

5. Eugene Peterson, *Subversive Spirituality* (Grand Rapids, Mich.: William B. Eerdmans, 1994, 1997), 13–14.

6. Brother David Steindl-Rast, *Gratefulness, the Heart of Prayer,* quoted in Helen Cordes and Jay Walljasper, eds., *Goodlife* (Minneapolis: Utne Reader, 1997), 127.

7. Rick Hamlin, *Finding God on the A Train* (San Francisco: Harper San Francisco, 1997), 4.

8. Thomas Howard, *An Antique Drum* (Philadelphia: J. B. Lippincott, 1969), 39, 44–45.

9. George Greenstein, quoted in Shirley O. Corriher, *Cookwise* (New York: William Morrow, 1997), 3.

10. Peter Reinhart, quoted in Shirley O. Corriher, *Cookwise* (New York: William Morrow, 1997), 3.

11. Wendell Berry, "The Politics of Supper," *Goodlife*, 161.

12. John Calvin, *Institutes*, I.5.1.

13. Eugene H. Peterson, *Leap Over a Wall* (San Francisco: Harper San Francisco, 1997), 85–86.

14. Rainer Maria Rilke, quoted in Ken Gire, *Windows of the Soul* (Grand Rapids, Mich.: Zondervan, 1996), 29.

15. Eugene Peterson, *Subversive Spirituality* (Grand Rapids, Mich.: William B. Eerdmans, 1994, 1997), 13–14.

16. Elizabeth Barrett Browning, "Aurora Leigh," 1857.

Chapter 5

THE SOUL AND THE SIMPLE LIFE

1. Bernd Heinrich, *A Year in the Maine Woods* (Reading, Mass.: Addison-Wesley, 1994), 70.

2. Henri Nouwen, *The Genesee Diary* (Garden City, N.Y.: Doubleday, 1976), 58–59.

3. Thomas Kelly, *A Testament of Devotion* (New York: Harper & Row, 1941), 114.

4. Ibid., 117.

5. Marjorie Thompson, *Soul Feast* (Louisville, Ky.: Westminster/John Knox, 1995), 1.

6. Thomas Merton, *Thoughts in Solitude* (Boston: Shambhala, 1956, 1958), 37.

7. E. B. White, *Essays of E. B. White,* quoted in Bob Benson, Sr., and Michael W. Benson, *Disciplines for the Inner Life* (Nashville: Thomas Nelson, 1989), 296.

8. Katy Butler, "Discontent Robs You of Your Life," quoted in Helen Cordes and Jay Walljasper, eds., *Goodlife* (Minneapolis: Utne Reader, 1997), 127.

9. Richard Foster, *Celebration of Simplicity* (San Francisco: Harper & Row, 1981), 143.

Chapter 6

EVERYDAY RHYTHMS

1. Stephan Rechtschaffen, *Timeshifting* (New York: Doubleday, 1996), 2.

2. Eugene Peterson, *The Wisdom of Each Other* (Grand Rapids, Mich.: Zondervan, 1998), 79.

3. Teresa of Avila, *The Way of Perfection* (New York: Image/Doubleday, 1964), 204.

4. John Dalrymple, *Simple Prayer* (Wilmington, Del.: Michael Glazier, 1984), 13, quoted in Richard Foster, *Coming Home* (San Francisco: Harper San Francisco, 1994).

5. Thomas Merton, *Thoughts in Solitude* (Boston: Shambhala, 1956, 1958), 62–64.

6. Howard Thurman, *The Inward Journey,* quoted in Bob Benson, Sr., and Michael W. Benson, *Disciplines for the Inner Life* (Nashville, Thomas Nelson, 1989), 68.

Chapter 7

WAKING UP TO MORE THAN A JOB

1. Marsha Sinetar, *To Build the Life You Want, Create the Work You Love* (New York: St. Martin's, 1995), 7.

2. Mihaly Csikszentmihalyi, *Finding Flow* (New York: Basic/HarperCollins, 1997), 9–10.

3. Frederick Buechner, quoted in Robert Benson, *Between the Dreaming and the Coming True* (San Francisco: Harper San Francisco, 1996), 76.

4. Oswald Chambers, *My Utmost for His Highest* (Uhrichsville, Ohio: Barbour, 1935, 1963), 50.

5. Cynthia Tobias, "Money Matters," Tape 1914, Christian Financial Concepts, Gainesville, Georgia.

6. Jean-Pierre de Caussade, *The Sacrament of the Present Moment,* trans. Kitty Muggeridge (New York: Harper & Row, 1981), 20.

7. Thomas Kelly, *A Testament of Devotion* (New York: Harper & Row, 1941).

8. Joan Chittister, O.S B., *Wisdom Distilled from the Daily* (San Francisco: Harper & Row, 1990), 13.

Chapter 8

SOUL COMPANIONS

1. Thomas Merton, *New Springs of Contemplation* (Notre Dame, Ind.: Ave Maria, 1992), 18.

2. Gerald Early, "The Frailty of Human Friendship," *Hungry Mind Review,* Winter 1996/97, 6.

3. Eugene Peterson, *Over the Wall* (San Francisco: Harper San Francisco, 1987), 53.

4. Quoted in Letty Cottin Pogrebin, *Among Friends* (New York: McGraw Hill, 1986), 4.

5. C. S. Lewis, *The Four Loves* (New York: Harcourt Brace Jovanovich, 1960), 96, quoted in Thomas Gillespie, "Theological Friendships," *The Princeton Theological Seminary Bulletin*, vol. xix, no. 1 (1998), 4.

6. Jay McInerney, "Raymond Carver: A Still, Small Voice," *New York Times Book Review*, August 6, 1989, 24.

7. Benedicta Ward, trans., *The Sayings of the Desert Fathers* (Kalamazoo, Mich.: Cistercian Publications, 1975, 84), 179–80.

8. Eugene Peterson, "The Summer of My Discontent," *Christianity Today*, January 15, 1990, 29–30.

9. Douglas Steere, *Together in Solitude* (New York: Crossroad, 1982), 33–34.

10. Eugene Peterson, *The Wisdom of One Another* (Grand Rapids, Mich.: Zondervan, 1998), 49.

11. Gerald May, *The Awakened Heart* (San Francisco: Harper San Francisco, 1991), 142.

Chapter 9

THE HARD, HIDDEN GRACES OF SUFFERING

1. Donald Hall, "The Porcelain Couple," *Without* (Boston: Houghton Mifflin, 1997), 13.

2. Quoted in Robert Benson, *Living Prayer* (New York: Jeremy Tarcher/Putnam, 1998), 49.

3. Elie Wiesel, *Night* (New York: Bantam, 1960), 64.

4. Jean-Pierre de Caussade, *The Sacrament of the Present Moment*, trans. Kitty Muggeridge (San Francisco: Harper & Row, 1981), 56.

5. C. S. Lewis, *The Problem of Pain* (New York: Macmillan, 1947), 81.

6. Peggy Noonan, "Looking Forward," *Good Housekeeping*, July 1996, 152.

7. Rebecca Faber, "A Mother's Grief Observed," "Parent Talk" (radio broadcast), January 14, 1998.

8. As told by Roberta Bondi, "Your Kingdom Come, Your Will Be Done," *Weavings*, March/April 1998, 11.

9. Origen of Alexandria, *Contra Celsus*, lxxii.

10. C. S. Lewis, *Mere Christianity* (New York: Collier/Macmillan, 1943, 1945, 1952), 38.

11. Simone Weil, *Waiting for God* (New York: Harper & Row, 1951), 89.

12. Anonymous journal entry, quoted in Christina Baldwin, *Life's Companion* (New York: Bantam Books, 1990), 22.

Chapter 10

FACING OUR FRAGILITY

1. Jay McInerney, *The Last of the Savages* (New York: Alfred A. Knopf, 1996), 3.

2. Michael Ingatieff, "Modern Dying," *The New Republic,* December 26, 1988, 28.

3. Frederick Buechner, *The Longing for Home* (San Francisco: Harper San Francisco, 1996), 7.

4. Michael Korda, "Ordeal of a Lucky Man," *Reader's Digest,* August 1996, 203.

5. Annie Dillard, *The Writing Life* (New York: Harper & Row, 1989), 41–42.

6. Thomas Lynch, *The Undertaking* (New York: W. W. Norton, 1997), 20–21.

Chapter 11

AWAKE TO THE FACES AROUND US

1. Sue Monk Kidd, "Live Welcoming to All," *Weavings,* September/October 1997, 8–9.

2. Susan Muto, *Late Have I Loved Thee* (New York: Crossroad, 1995), 25.

3. C. S. Lewis, *The Weight of Glory* (New York: Macmillan, 1949, 1975, 1980), 17.

4. Quoted in Philip Yancey, *What's So Amazing About Grace?* (Grand Rapids, Mich.: Zondervan, 1997), 280.

5. Fyodor Dostoevsky, quoted in Helmut Thielicke, *The Waiting Father* (New York: Harper and Brothers, 1959), 81.

6. Suggested by Eugene Peterson, *The Wisdom of Each Other* (Grand Rapids, Mich.: Zondervan, 1998), 45.

7. Quoted in William F. Schulz, fund-raising letter from Amnesty International, December 1997, Amnesty International USA, 322 Eighth Avenue, New York, NY 10001.

8. Eugene Peterson, *Reversed Thunder* (San Francisco: Harper & Row, 1988), 145.

9. Recounted in George H. Gallup, Jr., and Timothy Jones, *The Saints Among Us* (Ridgefield, Conn.: Morehouse, 1992), 51.

10. Attributed to Karl Barth, quoted in Jan Milac Lochman, "The Lord's Prayer in Our Time: Praying and Drumming," *The Princeton Seminary Bulletin,* Supplementary Issue No. 2, 1992, 19.

11. Sue Monk Kidd, "Birthing Compassion," *Weavings,* November/December 1990, 20.

12. Elise Miller Davis, "I Need You," *Woman's Day,* March 1972, 160.

Chapter 12

BY FITS AND STARTS

1. Saint Augustine, *Confessions,* trans. Henry Chadwick (Oxford, Eng.: Oxford University Press, 1991), 201.

2. Frederick Buechner, *The Longing for Home* (San Francisco: Harper San Francisco, 1996), 18–19.

3. Sue Monk Kidd, *When the Heart Waits* (San Francisco: Harper San Francisco, 1990), 22.

4. Simone Weil, *Waiting for God* (New York: Harper & Row, 1951), 112.

5. Henri Nouwen, *With Open Hands* (Notre Dame, Ind.: Ave Maria, 1972), 57.

6. Robert C. Morris, "The Second Breath," *Weavings,* March/April 1998, 42–43.

7. As told in Timothy Jones, "Frederick Buechner's Sacred Journey," *Christianity Today,* October 8, 1990, 51–52.